Michael Hinojosa's leadership of Dallas Independent School District (DISD) brought the board, the staff, and the community together around his vision for a high performing urban, low income, school district in Dallas. Then he led that district to accomplish what most thought was not possible—DISD was transformed to a high performing school system.

—Jack Lowe Jr.,
President & board member, DISD
Dallas, Texas

Hinojosa's experiences, shared in Superintendent-Wise, *provide a comprehensive field guide for school superintendents. Whether you are new to the superintendency or an experienced leader, this book is packed with valuable lessons and innovative approaches to tackle the daily challenges of leading school districts. A must-read for anyone committed to educational leadership and excellence.*

—Joe Gothard,
Superintendent, Madison Metropolitan School District
Madison, Wisconsin

My colleague and dear friend, Michael Hinojosa, is an incredibly gifted leader, having led more school districts in more states for more years than any of his contemporaries. For good reason, we call him the G.O.A.T. This book succinctly documents the secrets to his success and how his leadership evolved over the years. Aspiring superintendents as well as current district CEOs would do well to heed his model and advice.

—Barbara M. Jenkins,
Chief in Residence, CHIEFS FOR CHANGE
Winter Garden, Florida

In this book Hinojosa shows his unique ability to cut through the noise and get to the core principles that made him one of education's greatest leaders. His experience, insights, and perspective make this a must read.

—Bill Macatee,
Broadcaster
Dallas, Texas

Michael Hinojosa has gathered a lifetime's worth of insights into a single volume. This should be essential reading for both aspiring and seasoned school superintendents. He addresses all facets of public education leadership, enriching the text with a narrative that is captivating and thought-provoking. This work should be read and reread by anyone serious about making a positive difference in the lives of children.

—Michael Casserly,
Former Executive Director, Council of the Great City Schools
Washington, D.C.

As a fellow superintendent, I can attest to the incredible insights Michael Hinojosa offers in his book. His wealth of experience and practical advice make it an essential read for anyone dedicated to making a lasting impact in education. Hinojosa's strategies for navigating the complexities of the superintendency are both inspiring and actionable.

—Alberto M. Carvalho,
Superintendent, Los Angeles Unified School District
Los Angeles, California

Hinojosa has compiled an incredibly helpful, straightforward overview of lessons to assist leaders in succeeding in one of the most difficult jobs in the U.S.—that of an urban public school superintendent. It's an incredibly impactful role if done well, and it's one where quality onboarding is often lacking. I'm hopeful this book will accelerate the success of countless district leaders across the U.S.

—Todd Williams,
Chairman and CEO, The Commit Partnership
Dallas, Texas

SUPERINTENDENT-WISE

SUPERINTENDENT-WISE

CRITICAL LESSONS FOR LEADING YOUR DISTRICT

MICHAEL HINOJOSA

CORWIN

For information:

Corwin
A Sage Company
2455 Teller Road
Thousand Oaks, California 91320
(800) 233-9936
www.corwin.com

Sage Publications Ltd.
1 Oliver's Yard
55 City Road
London EC1Y 1SP
United Kingdom

Sage Publications India Pvt. Ltd.
Unit No 323-333, Third Floor, F-Block
International Trade Tower Nehru Place
New Delhi 110 019
India

Sage Publications Asia-Pacific Pte. Ltd.
18 Cross Street #10-10/11/12
China Square Central
Singapore 048423

Printed in the United States of America

Paperback ISBN 978-1-0719-1351-2

This book is printed on acid-free paper.

Vice President and Editorial Director:
    Monica Eckman
Acquisitions Editor: Pam Berkman
Content Development Manager:
    Desirée A. Bartlett
Development Editor: Sara Johnson
Senior Editorial Assistant:
    Nyle De Leon
Production Editor: Vijayakumar
Copy Editor: Terri Paulsen
Typesetter: TNQ Tech Pvt. Ltd.
Proofreader: Girish Kumar Sharma
Indexer: TNQ Tech Pvt. Ltd.
Cover Designer: Gail Buschman
Marketing Manager: Melissa Duclos

24 25 26 27 28 10 9 8 7 6 5 4 3 2 1

Contents

· ·

3. Nurture Excellence in Your Staff 47

4. Build Community Relations and Transparent Performance Management Systems 69

7. Cultivate All Endeavors on a Foundation of Ethics and Equity 113

Conclusion 125

Acknowledgments

I t gives me great pleasure to give specific acknowledgments to some key people in my career, which is my life. None of this would have been possible without the love of La Familia. La Familia is a group text chat that involves my wife, Kitty, and my three sons, Alex, Mike, and Taylor. All four of them are much smarter than me but we all click together. We spent every weekend together on the baseball diamonds of Texas and many other states. Now we spend every holiday together due to the unconditional love we have for each other. The text thread started with the Dallas Mavericks and now keeps us connected daily.

To my brother Joel Hinojosa, he taught me the power of relationships. He is the most connected person I have ever met. He is so generous that he exposed me and my brothers and sisters to things we would have never experienced. My sister Martha Hinojosa-Nadler taught me how to be disciplined in every sense of the word. My father was a pastor, and he taught me the power of storytelling with enthusiasm and humor.

Dr. Marvin Crawford, who promoted me from assistant principal to assistant superintendent in four short years, taught me how to be tenacious. Jack Lowe, the best board member I ever worked with, exemplified empathy and humility. There were three management gurus who helped me so much in my career. Tom Peters taught me about innovation. John Kotter taught me about transformation. And finally, Stephen Covey taught me about seven habits of highly effective people.

Any modicum of success I have had can be attributed to my drive and hunger while standing on the shoulders of these giants.

Publisher's Acknowledgments

Corwin gratefully acknowledges the contributions of the following reviewers:

Peter Dillon
Superintendent, Berkshire Hills Regional School District
Stockbridge, Massachusetts

Jill Gildea
Superintendent, Park City School District
Park City, Utah

Shelley Jallow
New York State Monitor, East Ramapo School District
Camden, New Jersey

Lynn Macan
Retired Superintendent, Cobleskill-Richmondville CSD
Bluffton, South Dakota

Dana Salles Trevethan
Superintendent, Turlock Unified
Turlock, California

About the Author

Dr. Michael Hinojosa served more than twenty-seven years as a superintendent/CEO of six public education systems, including two of the twenty-five largest school systems in the United States, Dallas Independent School District in Texas and the Cobb County School District in suburban Atlanta, Georgia. His career in public education, from teacher and coach to superintendent, spans more than four decades. He retired from the Dallas ISD in June 2022 after a long career in public education.

With a firm belief that education and not environment is the key to a student's success, he has led several school districts to improved student achievement. Dr. Hinojosa's recognitions include being named 2002 Superintendent of the Year by the Texas Association of School Boards and 2005 Superintendent of the Year by the University of Texas at Austin. He was honored as Distinguished Alumnus by the College of Education at Texas Tech University and as the Outstanding Latino Educator by the Association of Latino Administrators and Superintendents in 2014.

In 2019, *D Magazine* named Dr. Hinojosa the "Best Public Official" in Dallas. The Council of the Great City Schools awarded him the Green-Garner Award, the highest honor in urban education, as the 2020 Urban Educator of the Year. Dr. Hinojosa is a recipient of the CoSN (Consortium for School Networking) and AASA (American Association of School Administrators) 2021 EmpowerED Digital Superintendent Award. In 2022, he received the Champion of Science and Medicine from the Dallas County Medical Society. He is also a past president of the Texas Association of School Administrators. He currently serves as Superintendent in Residence for both the Council of the Great City Schools and the Texas Urban Council.

Dr. Hinojosa, a proud graduate of Dallas ISD, holds a doctorate in education from the University of Texas at Austin. He has three sons, graduates of Texas Tech University, Harvard University, and Princeton University. All three attended Dallas ISD for a significant portion of their K–12 careers.

Introduction

People often ask me why I served as a superintendent for twenty-seven years. The answer is simple. But first, I need to tell you the story of my family. My parents had a formal fifth-grade education in the villages of Padilla and Jimenez in Northern Mexico. My dad wanted to date my mom, but she would not agree to date him unless he went to church. My dad was an orphan and had a bit of a wild streak, but he envied my mother's large family, so he eventually agreed.

After some time, my parents married, and my father became a minister. He and my mom taught themselves to read using the rigorous text of the Bible. They had ten children—five boys and five girls. My father wanted to move his family to the United States so they could get a great education. He kept accepting church assignments that would get him closer to the United States of America. I was the eighth child and the last one born in Mexico, in a modest house in Nuevo Laredo, Tamaulipas, a small town on the Mexico–United States border. When I was two years old, my father was awarded a minister position in Lubbock, Texas, in 1959, after the membership approved him by just one vote. I would later have a younger brother and sister, both born in Lubbock. Our huge family lived in an eight-hundred-square-foot home in East Lubbock.

My parents insisted that if we were going to make the sacrifice to be away from extended family it had better be worth it. So, they did everything in their power to ensure that we would do well in school. However, not all our schooling from Mexico transferred to the United States. My oldest two sisters had already been to a form of business school in middle years (equivalent to U.S. middle school) in Mexico, but the Lubbock Independent School District wanted to put them back in middle school despite them being fifteen and sixteen years old. Both became successful businesswomen. One became the tax assessor collector for the city of LaPorte, Texas. The other was an entrepreneur in San Antonio, Texas, where she ran a beauty shop in the Harlandale area of the city.

The rest of us all graduated from high school. In the 1970s, for a Latino family to have an 80 percent graduation rate among their kids was excellent by all accounts. Three of us went on to earn college degrees. But my parents' real legacy is that they have twenty-two grandchildren. Twenty of their grandchildren went to college and seventeen graduated with a bachelor's degree, including my three sons who graduated from Texas Tech University, Harvard, and

Princeton. The two grandchildren who did not attend college had special needs that prevented them from attending.

It is incredible to me the impact that school and education can have on the life of an individual—positive or negative—as well as on an entire family. My family is a walking testament to the positive effects. Just one generation removed from a life of poverty and immigration, through strong schools and my parents' desire for us to have more education, my siblings and I were able to graduate from high school and eventually send almost all grandchildren to college. Seeing the impact of education first-hand in the lives of my family and knowing how it can change a person's entire life trajectory is why I became a superintendent and educator; I've loved every minute of it.

The lessons I learned as a superintendent are nothing like what I learned in the classroom or even as a building administrator. Sure, there are skills like flexibility, time management, and adaptability that cross over, but the actual job of being a superintendent, especially in a large urban district, requires skills and understanding that I only learned the longer I lived in that role. It is for that reason that I sought to share these lessons with others through this book in the hopes that I can help you lead your urban district more effectively and more positively impact the lives of the students and families you serve.

A friend of mine once had to introduce me to a crowd before a speaking engagement. Unknowingly, she gave me one of the biggest compliments of my career. She introduced me as "the unapologetic Michael Hinojosa." She is right, I am unapologetic about who I am. I am proud to be an immigrant, I am proud to be from the hood, *Oak Cliff!* I close every speech with the past, the present, and the future. Be proud of your past and never apologize for it. You are a product of your lived experiences, and you are a successful human being. In the present, be present—nothing great happens in the absence of enthusiasm. Look to the future with hope and aspiration. I am an optimistic person and I believe in the art of the possible! That is me: *unapologetic!*

How This Book Is Structured

In **Chapter 1**, I explain the importance of working with the school board. I also share the Success Triangle (see Figure 1.1) and how it can be used as a framework for balancing relationships and time management as a superintendent. As part of working with the school board, I also share strategies for a successful entry plan that can help ensure new superintendents hit the ground running.

Chapter 2 shares lessons learned from navigating the waters of media and politics. As superintendents in large, urban districts, by default we must learn to play the media and politics game or we won't be around long enough to affect any kind of positive change for our students and staff. Whether it's in our day-to-day activities or during a crisis, the relationships we build with the media and government play a role in our effectiveness as a leader; the strategies and tips I share can help you stay in the driver's seat.

In **Chapter 3**, I share methods for identifying and nurturing excellence in your staff. Since human capital typically makes up approximately 80 percent of a school district budget, it is important to have the right people doing the right jobs. This will allow you to be a more effective leader who might even find time to think about strategically passing the torch one day.

In **Chapter 4**, I share how community relations and performance management—two things that people don't normally think of as being related—can work together to build relationships, promote trust and transparency, and transform school districts.

Chapter 5 begins with a discussion of a school district's theory of action: its value proposition. As district leaders, we must ensure that our districts remain focused on academic expectations, academic systems, and professional learning. However, if things fall off track or you step into a position with schools not performing to expectation, I share turnaround strategies and lessons learned from my experiences.

Chapter 6 takes a high-level view of operations. As a superintendent, especially a new superintendent, it can be intimidating to suddenly oversee so many more operational departments than when you were a building administrator. Having a high-level understanding of the purpose and function of each department can get you started so that you have a sense of the scope and can strategically choose where to focus attention more deeply.

In **Chapter 7**, we conclude with a discussion about ethics and equity. Although this could have easily been the first chapter of the book, we conclude with it as a reminder that ethics and equity is a foundation for everything else that we do. Without these, we can't expect to be effective leaders or positively affect change in our districts. You can't just talk about equity; you have to deliver.

Features in This Book

▶ **Pro Tips:** Quick and practical ideas born from my experiences.

▶ **Hinojosa-isms:** These are sayings and phrases I say all the time. I may not have been the first to say them, but I've repeated them so many times it feels like it!

▶ **Sidebars:** The sidebars contain helpful information, such as definitions or added info for extra context.

▶ **The Big Ideas:** At the end of each chapter, you will find a bulleted list recapping the chapter's main takeaways.

▶ **Reflect and Act:** Please take the time to journal your thoughts and reflections at the end of each chapter. The Reflect and Act worksheet asks you to consider five As: what you agree with, what you would argue with, how you might apply the learning in your own district, and what actions you can take in your district and how you might hold yourself accountable for following through on those actions.

Let's get started!

CHAPTER 1

Prioritize Board Relations

I served as superintendent and chief executive officer in six different communities over the course of twenty-seven years. Among the many lessons I learned, the most important was how to work effectively with the school board.

My First Lesson

In the summer of 1994, before becoming superintendent in Fabens Independent School District (ISD), I was serving as the assistant superintendent in Grand Prairie Independent School District, a Dallas suburb. Much to my own surprise as a kid from the 'hood, I thrived in this suburban education environment, rising from a high school assistant principal to the superintendent's right-hand man in less than four years. The superintendent was a hard-charging leader with a "take no prisoners" mindset, and I think that he identified me for promotion because I was very much the same. My stubborn, intense, and direct demeanor motivated me to make something of myself. Coming from the inner-city, where you always must watch your back, I had learned to subscribe to the idea that "if you're not with me, you're against me." In the streets of Oak Cliff or on the pick-up basketball courts of West Dallas, any slights—real or perceived—had to be answered forcefully. Trying to make peace was often seen as a sign of weakness. These traits might have made for a good assistant superintendent attack dog, viciously protecting the man who rapidly promoted me, but they didn't make for a good strategic leader and decision-maker.

This was never more evident than when I devised a plan to deal with a particularly pesky teacher and labor leader. The superintendent's support from the school board had begun to wane, and the head of a local teacher organization, who was the planetarium instructor at one of the district's two high schools, started publicly criticizing the superintendent at every school board meeting. After one particularly brutal board meeting, the superintendent asked me—as the head of human resources—what certifications this teacher possessed. When I found out that he was dually certified in math and science, we vindictively decided to reassign him to an open position at the district's toughest middle school.

This response was not the wisest of choices. Rather than considering what we could do to mend the divide with this influential teacher and community member, we instead reacted negatively and turned someone who had a good-faith policy dispute into a permanent enemy. The teacher was understandably upset and filed a formal grievance against the superintendent. Although the administration's decision was upheld, our reactive decision-making was wrong on both ethical and strategic levels. Unsatisfied, the teacher filed a lawsuit against the district, which resulted in a small out-of-court settlement covering only attorney's fees. Naïvely, we thought that was the last of it. Instead of accepting the settlement as the end of the matter, the teacher decided to run for school board himself and won. Reading the writing on the wall, the superintendent and I knew it was time to leave the district. By seeking to stifle the dissent we feared would poison the board against us, our shortsighted and stubborn reactivity directly caused the situation we were trying to avoid. It's not what happens to you, it's how you respond, and we responded poorly.

This story illustrates how complex it is to work in the public sector with elected officials. Over time, I learned lessons about what to do and what not to do by observing the actions of people I respected. Eventually, with support from a former successful superintendent at Spring Independent School District, I developed what I called the Success Triangle.

Hinojosa-ism

It's not what happens to you, it's how you respond.

Bad things happen to good people. Good things happen to bad people. Being responsible is about having the ability to respond to the situation appropriately.

The Success Triangle

The Success Triangle (see Figure 1.1) is the idea that all parts of the school community— particularly the school board, the community, and the teachers and staff—are interconnected and serve to meet the needs of the students. The superintendent's job is to maintain a balance so that the needs of one group do not outweigh any of the others and they all work in concert to keep the district functioning properly. In the middle of the triangle are the students. They are your primary customers. All products and services should be aligned so that student achievement outcomes are the highest priority of the entire system.

Figure 1.1   The Success Triangle

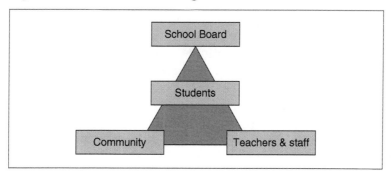

At the top of the triangle is the school board, which in most public education systems is elected by the public. *They are your bosses; you are not their boss.* The board members come from different walks of life and professional backgrounds, and they often do not have the same educational training and experiences as the administration. In most states the school board has three major functions.

Functions of a School Board

1. Adopt a budget as recommended by the superintendent.

2. Adopt policies that will govern and oversee the management of the school system.

3. Hire and/or fire the chief executive officer, also known as the superintendent of schools.

In one corner of the triangle are the teachers and staff. The staff is made up of a diverse array of positions, including direct reports to the superintendent, central office staff, and campus staff who are key to implementing strategy and ensuring positive educational outcomes for students.

In the other corner of the triangle is the community, which is also very diverse. Every member of the community has experience with schooling, whether it be public or private. Adult members of the community pay taxes that fund the school system, and many entrust the school system with the education of their own children.

It is imperative that the superintendent have strong relationships with all groups in the Success Triangle. If all three parts of the triangle are balanced, then student achievement outcomes will be significant and great opportunities for students and families will be developed and implemented. The district and the superintendent will thrive. If all three parts of the triangle are not balanced, then the district and the superintendent may be able to survive, but probably not for long. As an example, if the board and staff love the superintendent but the community does not like specific district policies, then one school board election could change everything. School board elections typically have the lowest turnouts of any elected office. Thus, it takes fewer voters to change who sits on the board. If the superintendent does not have support from all three corners of the Success Triangle, it's very possible that separation from employment will become imminent.

PRO TIP

Color-code your calendar to make sure you're spending time with each key segment of the Success Triangle.

I applied that learning to my leadership strategy for the balance of my career. My calendar became color-coded, with each portion of the triangle represented by a different color. Because I was strategic in this approach and did not micromanage my direct reports, I was able to spend quality time with my family and exercise regularly. I learned that it was my job to coach rather than play in each portion of the triangle, which helped me create a work–life balance. In this chapter I share strategies that I hope will help you in developing productive relationships with school board members. Chapters 2 and 4 offer strategies for developing productive relationships with members of the community, and Chapter 3 offers strategies for developing productive relationships with staff.

Making a Positive Start

It is often extremely difficult to get hired as a superintendent. Among a sea of applicants, approximately five to seven are selected for an interview but only one candidate gets hired. Most boards understand that this is a recruitment and selection process much beyond an interview. The interview and presentation are important, but more significant is the body of actual work accomplished.

Customer Intimacy

A marketing and relationship-building strategy where brands work to acquire extensive knowledge about their customers, and then use that data to meet their customers' needs in unique and personalized ways.

As a candidate, do your due diligence. Have a strong understanding of who the people are on the hiring committee and gather important information about the district, particularly quantitative data. Customer intimacy, although an unconventional term in the world of education, is critical. A candidate should know more about the district than the incumbent board members. Building relationships with your board members starts preemployment. As a candidate, I was always very clear and transparent about what is important to me. I would give them answers to the questions I knew they wanted to ask but couldn't.

Create an Organic Entry Plan

The preemployment research pays off once you are hired and begin to develop an entry plan. An entry plan is designed to help superintendents who are new to a community systematically collect information about their new school district. But don't make the mistake of executing an entry plan off the shelf. It needs to come about organically, as the key players in every district are different.

I learned about the power of an entry plan from Dr. Marvin Crawford—the man who gave me my first job in school district administration, and Tony Trujillo, a former superintendent of Ysleta Independent School District, who taught me that you get power by giving it away. With these lessons in mind, I developed a robust entry plan that allowed me to identify the people with whom I need to build consensus. I carry this strategy with me to every new job I take.

Most superintendents come into a new job overwhelmed, especially when they are not promoted from within. Oftentimes, their entry plans are totally scripted because they think they already know exactly what needs to be done, or they are generic and scattershot because they have no idea what to do. Mine is focused and research based, with the intent to build consensus in three months. It requires patience, precision, and discipline. It is hard work, but the payoff is significant.

I implemented my first entry plan when I took my first job as superintendent, at Fabens Independent School District, a tiny district outside of El Paso, Texas. Implementing it only took thirty days because the district was so small. As I implemented entry plans in other districts, my system evolved. The basic premise behind my entry plan is to conduct an interactive, qualitative analysis of the status of the district. Quantitative data in any district is plentiful—there are accountability reports, financial and program audits, and depending on the quality of the research department there could be many evaluation reports that are readily available. But what is typically not available are the stories behind the numbers. When you are new on the job, I urge you to ask the questions that will mitigate the false positives that emerge when only focusing on the numbers.

In smaller districts, I met with thirty people in thirty days. In the first week you can unpack, get acclimated to the new surroundings, and meet all the school board members. In the second week you can meet with all direct reports to the superintendent and all principals. In the next two weeks schedule meetings with the remaining stakeholders. In medium-size districts, I met with sixty people in sixty days; in large districts, I met with one hundred people in one hundred days. In every district, I met with each trustee individually, starting with the board president. Then, I met with the direct reports to the superintendent. To each meeting I would bring a one-page document with blank spaces next to prompts such as "Education," "Work History," "Family," "Hobbies," and "Interests." I would fill out the document during our conversation and keep it on hand so that I could remember them better in future encounters. The goal of the meeting would be to build relationships and a personal connection. In smaller districts, I met with every principal. In larger districts, I met with a sampling of the principals and key department heads. Toward the end of the process, I met with leaders of employee groups, key community leaders such as the mayor, and key elected officials.

In every system I used the same first five questions to help me identify where the district is, where it should go, and the people who could help me get there.

Key Questions to Ask Stakeholders

1. What is the most important expectation you have of the superintendent?

2. If you were in my shoes, what would you focus on first?

3. What three things do we have to do to make this the best district in the county, city, or state?

4. Who are the most respected people on staff and why?

5. Who are the external stakeholders that are critical to our future success?

The first three questions are similar but worded in three different ways to avoid false positives. They help identify high-priority issues that are top of mind to key leaders. These items that emerge require attention early on. Questions four and five are power questions. They identify the internal and external leaders who will be crucial when making consensus decisions. Depending on circumstances in a particular district, additional questions can be developed if certain matters require specific attention. Strategy and focus become extremely obvious if the process is followed rigorously. Doing this when you start your job as superintendent (aka chief executive officer) in your community will help you expand your circle of influence and narrow your circle of concern. If you believe in consensus decision-making, this strategy will help you identify the internal and external stakeholders that will help you make and implement your most important decisions. Figure 1.2 includes guidance to help you plan for these meetings.

Figure 1.2 Organic Entry Plan Essentials

People to meet with in the first three months	Materials to gather in advance of each meeting
• Each board member, beginning with the chair • All direct reports to the superintendent • Key department heads • Random sampling of principals • Teacher leaders, especially of labor organizations • Community leaders, such as the mayor	• Research on everything about them personally and professionally • A one-page document with prompts next to blank spaces to get to know them on a personal level (this applies to all employees) • Conduct an internet search to find relevant stories in the media

To get acquainted with your district, make a plan to meet with the following people:

▶ Each school board trustee individually, starting with the board president and working through the officers

▶ Your direct team (superintendent direct reports), reviewing their one-page document prior to the meeting

▶ All principals (small districts) or a sampling of principals and key department heads (larger districts)

▶ Leaders of employee groups and important community leaders such as the mayor and key elected officials

Have a goal of meeting people to help get acclimated and learn as much as you can about the district—thirty people in thirty days (small districts), sixty people in sixty days (medium-sized districts), and one hundred people in one hundred days (large districts). Every school board that hired me was extremely complimentary of my discipline to execute this entry plan. I typically reported the results to the board in public before the end of the hundred days.

Accept Responsibility and Solve Problems

Unless you are the very first superintendent of a new school district, you will inevitably inherit situations from your predecessor. I inherited several scandals in my first few years in Dallas Independent School District. Resolutions to those matters had to be implemented before stability set in.

One scandal in particular stands out. In 2008, my chief of staff told me that our chief operations officer (COO) had just informed him that there was a significant problem with the district's annual budget. The COO had been very successful with numerous businesses and was hired because the Operations Division had been by far the weakest division in the school district. While well-intentioned and clearly competent in his former roles, the COO did not understand government accounting and was in over his head regarding school finance. But he was too proud to admit it.

The district found itself facing a $64 million deficit and only had $32 million in the reserve account. It became clear to me that the COO had no understanding of just how precarious the situation was when he told me that this represented "only" 5 percent of our annual budget. As a numbers person who had spent the preceding twenty-five years in school district administration, the stakes were immediately apparent to me. Unlike at the federal level, municipal governments are unable to engage in deficit spending to finance operational expenses. Instead, every dollar must be accounted for and the district's revenue—in the form of property taxes and funding received from the state based on student population—can never fall below its obligated spending. Unlike a private business that could have covered a 5 percent deficit by seeking a line of credit, such a shortfall would have sent the district into complete insolvency, with disastrous consequences for the city and the community.

In the event of a school district not being able to meet its financial obligations to employees and vendors, the state has the power to take it over entirely. If we did not act fast, the Texas Education Agency would have appointed a master and a board of managers—essentially removing all authority from myself as superintendent and the school board as representatives of the community—to make the necessary changes to put the district back on firm financial footing. As this distressing reality washed over me, I realized that I had two choices: I could immediately resign in disgrace, or I could stay in my position and deal with the difficult reality of fixing the budget no matter how unpopular I became. I chose the latter because I believe it's not what happens to you, it's how you respond that determines your destiny.

My chief of staff and I moved into action immediately. I dismissed the COO, and within three hours the two of us worked through the problem and found a solution that we knew would be extraordinarily painful but had to be done. We determined that the shortfall was not the result of any malfeasance or corruption but instead it was the product of a patchwork bureaucratic system that had been haphazardly rolling along for decades. No money was missing or stolen; instead, the district had been over-hiring for years. Most districts have systems called "position controls," which ensure that each position is adequately funded. Dallas lacked these systems, and hiring decisions were made based on appeals to our budgeting director by understaffed principals. Over time, the slow drip of over-hiring had become a tsunami that threatened to wash away a key entity of the Dallas community. There was not one villain, but instead a system that was in desperate need of modernization.

Before we could address the underlying problem, we had to stop the flood with what we knew would be a painful solution—we had to lay off a thousand employees, mostly teachers. The only way to do so would be for the school board to declare financial exigency—announcing to the world that we were broke. Without it, we could not have broken contracts and laid off staff. I could have felt sorry for myself, pointed fingers, and played the victim. But I knew that my resignation would only serve to throw the district into chaos and delay the ultimate, inescapable solution. I knew that this move would understandably anger the board and the community and that, as the man at the top of the chain of command, I would have to shoulder the blame. I could have shrunk from the fight, but I knew that the district that had given me my education and the opportunity to change the trajectory of my family's story was more important than my ego.

As the superintendent and CEO, the buck stopped with me. I could not shirk my responsibilities. My staff could have delivered the news to the board, but I couldn't let others do the dirty work for me. I had my chief of staff invite our senior staff to my office where I laid out the problem and the painful solution. I called my wife and asked her to tell my family about the problem and then personally called each board member to describe the problem and let them know that I already had a solution, even if it was an extremely difficult one.

I called a news conference for that very afternoon to reveal my findings to the media, and in turn the staff and the community.

This kicked off the most stressful period of my professional career. My adrenaline kicked in and I immediately went into problem-solving mode. Over the course of the next several weeks, I lost significant weight. I had no appetite, and I didn't go out in public as much as before. Prominent members of the community and the local media started to question my leadership. For weeks, I had to wake my boys up early on Saturday mornings so we could leave our house before scores of protesters showed up demanding my resignation. Rather than feeling sorry for myself, I knew that responsibility is the ability to choose your response.

Over the next few months, we kept in constant communication with the school board and carried out our plan with single-minded intensity and focus. Our plan involved

▶ immediately reducing overstaffing and preparing a balanced budget for the next year,

▶ hiring the best chief financial officer in the state who had fixed similar situations in two other high-profile districts in Texas and giving him total autonomy and authority, and

▶ changing the audit firm we worked with to one that would identify Material Weaknesses and Significant Deficiencies and create a plan to resolve the matter long term, especially regarding position control.

We understood the pain that it would cause, but we also understood that it had to be done. Slowly but surely, we got the budget under control and stabilized the district, which enabled us to rehire more than six hundred of the one thousand employees that we were forced to let go as vacancies opened naturally throughout the district. This time, however, we did so with systems in place that allowed us to be sure that a crisis like this would never happen again. By the end of the school year, we turned a $64 million deficit into a $30 million surplus. In fact, by the end of my second tenure as superintendent of Dallas ISD, in 2022, the district had never been financially stronger, with more than $700 million in reserves. Our newfound financial stability allowed us to deal with numerous other crises that arose during my second superintendency—from a vicious tornado that destroyed three of our schools to the COVID-19 pandemic, where we successfully got computers and broadband access to 145,000 low-income students as we were all forced into remote learning.

The lessons I had internalized earlier gave me the tools I needed to face the worst moment of my professional career. It is not what happens to you, it is how you respond. The school board let me stay and, in fact, most of the same board rehired me in 2015 because I took responsibility and I communicated with them directly.

Strategies for Building Positive Relationships With Board Members

It would be an oversimplification to say that the school board hires those they like and fires those they don't, but there is a kernel of truth there. To lead effectively, it is essential to build positive relationships with all the board members. When you have strong, positive relationships with the school board members, they are more likely to offer grace and extend flexibility to you as you correct your mistakes or work through challenging circumstances. Faulty relationships with board members can lead to mistrust, unnecessary scrutiny, judgment, and potentially even public exposure or embarrassment. Being able to survive a significant crisis is based upon many hours of building significant capital with school board members over time. It is too late to start the process when the crisis emerges.

Hinojosa-ism

The school board hires those they like and fires those they don't.

Dr. Bob Thompson runs a superintendents' academy. He is known to say, "If you are likeable, they will overlook many of your mistakes. If you are a jerk, they will look at every email, text, expense report and memo to find something to take you down."

My strategies for building positive relationships with school board members include (1) scheduling recurring meetings with the board president and other members, (2) planning off-site retreats for a deep review of a few items critical to future success, and (3) getting to know the personality types of the individual board members and the most effective strategies for communicating with people with those personality types. In the section below, I develop each of these ideas in more depth.

Hold Regular Meetings

The most significant relationship is with the board president or chairperson. Like it or not, this individual wields significant power. An easy way to build rapport with the board president is through regular meetings and interactions. These meetings enable communication, strategy building, and the exchange of general routine information. In my experience, the longer I was in the district or the longer the president served in their role, the less frequent the meetings became. Each president I worked with had a unique style. I found myself needing to learn and adapt so that I was using a communication style and approach that worked best with each one. For example, some wanted structured meetings in offices. Others wanted to meet in more casual settings, such as lunch or the occasional happy hour. And the meetings were not all business—we had conversations about topics of mutual interest such as sports, hobbies, and family. This helped to build trust and rapport and mutual respect for the work we each did to support the success of the school district.

Relationships with the board officers are also vital, especially with the ones who do not support you and are very public about it. I attempted to meet with each board member at least once every other month. These sessions should be routine, casual, and well-documented. They typically occurred over lunch, which I chose never to seek reimbursement for. I never felt it necessary for taxpayers' dollars to be used in this way. Very few, but some board members refused to meet with me, and I always felt it a good idea to document attempted meetings in case that information should ever be requested. The purpose of these meetings is to get to know what drives them personally and professionally and to determine if there are areas where you both agree and can jointly support. Some board members run for office and get elected on the board to drive a particular agenda. It is imperative that you are aware of those people and their agendas.

Clear and consistent communication is also critical to building effective relationships with school board members. During my twenty-seven years as a superintendent, I developed three types of communications that I sent to the board:

▶ *Board Update Report:* Sent weekly (typically on Friday mornings), these reports were intended to keep them apprised of key issues in the district and anticipated future issues.

▶ *Trustee Notices:* These emails were sent to the entire board only as needed when "hot issues" arose that might appear in the media. They were always generated by the chief of communications to ensure that the board members understood the matter was urgent.

▶ *Highly Urgent and Sensitive News:* When the news was big and bad, I and only I called each board member directly and would answer all their questions personally.

Another effective way to build relationships and rapport with the school board is to have members of the district leadership team serve as trustee liaisons. Not all members of the senior staff had the ability to work closely with board members, but those who did met regularly with the board to discuss key initiatives and to seek input on ideas. Each board member was assigned a specific chief (district leader) who would be their main point of contact. They would navigate the bureaucracy and meet with the trustee regularly, especially before board meetings, to answer their questions. Board members loved working with the trustee liaisons because it made them more effective as a result of their access to information and the relationships they formed with the liaisons. The selected chiefs enjoyed being "stretched" professionally and having actual experiences with elected officials. And because other district leaders were spending focused time with the trustees, it gave me more time to spend in the other parts of the Success Triangle. Seldom did I have to change the liaison once the relationships began. This distributive leadership strategy built the capacity of key leaders, many of whom later became superintendents. Depending on the size of the district, the behavior of the board members, and the capacity of my senior leaders, this strategy evolved over time. The confidence that I gained through experience allowed me to get more power by giving it away to key direct reports.

Create Off-Site Retreats

There was also power in having off-site retreats with the board. Despite having one board chair who did not believe in them, these sessions were very powerful. These are legally called meetings, which must follow posting requirements. But they are designed in a way in which no official proceedings or actions would be taken. There was always only a few items on the agenda—these were important but not urgent items for dialogue. This gave the board the opportunity to go into deep review of a few items that were critical to the future success of the school district. Goal setting, budget prioritization, preparing for significant referenda, and dreaming about the future would typically be the types of topics we discussed.

Tactical projects, such as creating or updating Board Operating Procedures, are also something that can be accomplished in a retreat setting. This type of manual or document outlines in writing the process, procedures, and protocols for most matters that a board will face, such as meeting procedures and individual board members' conduct. A written protocol will avoid confusion and will provide clarity for all board members.

PRO TIP

It is not the job of the superintendent to police the behavior of the board or its individual members. If the board does not handle this themselves, then there is nothing the superintendent can do about it.

Know Personality Styles

Knowing the personality style of each board member can also be extremely helpful in building strong relationships. There are many expensive products that will help identify personality styles in any group. There are also products that are not proprietary and rather simple to execute. The one I use puts members of the group into four quadrants: driver, expressive, analytical, and amiable. All four are very important in any group because they typically depend on the others to make better decisions. However, because these personality styles are so different, they sometimes do not appreciate the style of other personality types.

A *driver* typically wants action. The driver is dynamic and active. The driver is difficult to discourage. They are natural-born leaders who are typically visionary and at times could care less about details. In making a decision, the driver can be described as one who follows the sequence of ready, fire, aim. A driver wants action now and typically does not care for long-winded discussions. A driver makes things happen but makes mistakes because not all data in making the decision were considered. The feelings of people may not be considered. Building support and ownership are less of a priority, but decisions are made readily. Every team needs at least one driver, but it wouldn't be good to have a team made up only of drivers.

An *expressive* is the life of any party. They are outgoing. They are in every photo op. The expressive loves to have fun and is very charismatic and persuasive. In making a decision, the expressive follows the sequence of ready, aim, please take a picture of me before I fire. The expressive is often seen as shallow or undisciplined and loud. They are usually the champions for the group. They typically are the very vocal ambassadors for the team. Every team needs at least one expressive, but not all.

An *analytical* is the serious, thoughtful person who has very high standards and depends significantly on data. The analytical is orderly and organized and is intolerant of those who are not. In making a decision, the analytical follows the sequence of ready, aim, aim, aim, aim, and typically never fires because they do not have enough data. They are often seen as indecisive or uncooperative due to the constant number of questions they ask on every issue. They usually help the team make much better decisions due to the quality of the information they gather. Every team needs at least one analytical, but not all.

The *amiable* is sympathetic and empathetic. These individuals are quiet and are always concerned about how people will feel about the decision. They agonize about the impact of decisions on every stakeholder group. They are seen as gentle people who will avoid conflict at all costs. In making a decision, the amiable follows the sequence of ready, aim, oh *mijo*, please don't aim that gun. Can't we all just hold hands and sing "Kumbaya"? The amiable forces the team to consider the impact on people. They play a very powerful role. Every team needs at least one amiable, but not all.

Every team needs diversity in every sense of the word. The school board and the superintendent are a team. The superintendent should fill the void in the above-referenced team if a personality style is missing. Every superintendent has a preferred style, but you do not get to pick the school board. In fact, the board changes every time there is an election. A savvy superintendent is wise to take this into consideration.

Being a successful superintendent is not a linear endeavor. You have to do you, but it is not about you. The district is not your district. It belongs to the people who you serve—the school board, the staff, and the community—so that the students can be successful.

Hinojosa-ism

You have to do you, but it is not about you.

Be proud of who you are and where you come from. Never apologize for your set of experiences. But remember, you are here to serve the people you lead.

The Big Ideas

Being a successful superintendent means building relationships with the school board. Here are the big ideas I shared in Chapter 1:

- *Utilize the Success Triangle.* The Success Triangle is made up of the school board, the community, and the teachers and staff. The students are at the center. In order for the district to function and for you to do well in your job, all sections of the triangle must be balanced.

- *Know what you're getting into before you apply.* Do your due diligence and apply the concept of customer intimacy to get to know the board during the interview phase.

- *Create your entry plan organically.* Meet with board members, key district and school leaders, and community members and ask them qualitative questions to get the true story behind the quantitative data.

▶ *Get to know board members' personality styles.* It is much easier to be effective when you know who you're working with and how they like to work. And remember, as the makeup of the board changes, you will have to adapt how you work with them!

CHAPTER #1

Reflect and Act

Now it's time to reflect on what you've read and decide how you can best apply the insights gained from the chapter in practical ways within your district. Use this modified "five 'A's" protocol (Agree, Argue, Apply, Actions, and Accountable) to journal your ideas.

What do you **agree** with in the chapter?	What do you want to **argue** about within the chapter?
How can you **apply** the information from this chapter to your own district?	What **actions** can you take after reading this chapter? And how will you hold yourself **accountable**?

Adapted from Judith Gray, "Four 'A's Text Protocol," National School Reform Faculty (2005), www.nsrfharmony.org.

CHAPTER 2

Carefully Navigate the Waters of Media and Politics

In my personal and professional opinion, the second most challenging part of being a successful urban superintendent is navigating the media and politics. This fits in the community section of the Success Triangle; although some coverage can span the state or nation, it is often members of the local community with whom you are interacting with politically and who are consuming digital and media coverage about your school district.

Media relations are important and complex in small, rural, and suburban districts. However, in large city districts with a significant online media presence, media relations have a much stronger impact on the politics of the superintendent's position and often require a great deal more attention than in smaller districts. Based on my experience in both types of districts, I will share strategies that will help all superintendents navigate media and politics with success.

Understanding Media Relations

I stumbled upon a stark reality upon the announcement of my appointment as superintendent of Dallas ISD in the late spring of 2005. While I was extremely excited to be the hometown boy selected to lead the district that had trained me as a student and teacher, I felt a sinking feeling in the pit of my stomach when I looked out at the sea of cameras that were recording every word I said. I had over ten years of experience as a superintendent in other districts and had been interviewed on television numerous times, but I quickly realized that being the superintendent of a district in one of the largest media markets in the United States was going to be different than anything I had ever experienced before. Not all media coverage is created equal.

In the 1990s, Dallas ISD had a very negative reputation in the media due to a rapid succession of superintendents, including one who went to federal prison for abusing the district's credit cards. Additionally, significant racial tension and disagreement between the three major racial groups in the district negatively impacted the climate of this district so much that the business community, civic leaders, philanthropic organizations, and governmental entities refused to work with it. In 2001, the district began to turn things around by hiring the former Commissioner of Education in Texas, Dr. Mike Moses, as superintendent on a five-year contract. Dr. Moses stayed three-and-a-half years, and while progress had been made, the state of the district remained fragile. In my personal and professional opinion, he made the job doable.

Among the congratulatory phone calls I received was one from the CEO of the Dallas Citizens Council, which is a business organization made up of the CEOs of the major corporations in Dallas. The minority groups and leaders in the district were significantly suspicious of the Citizens Council because most members were White men who wielded significant power. However, the Citizens Council understood that it would not be good for business if the school district reverted to the ways of the mid-'90s.

During that call, the CEO offered to send the media specialist who had worked in the Reagan and Bush administrations to train me on media relations even before I started my tenure. I accepted the offer, and Merrie Spaeth videotaped me for two days in preparation for the onslaught of media interviews. In fact, on the advice of Dr. Moses, I did not speak to anyone publicly during the twenty-one-day lone finalist period. The review of the videos showed that my mustache twitched when the fake reporter asked me a tough question, and my eye wandered upward when I was thinking. Neither inspired confidence on camera. I also used negative words like *corrupt* instead of constructive words such as *accountability* when responding to questions. The experience launched my commitment to proactively correspond with the media.

The Importance of Focused Messaging

My training with the media specialist taught me the power of messaging. In the past, I had never used talking points because they seemed disingenuous. Authenticity is very important to me. Therefore, in my previous posts, I did not use teleprompters or prerehearsed talking points. To this day, when I speak publicly, I tell people to be proud of who they are and where they come from and to never apologize for it. That is why I wear my mustache and hair the way I do. However, the training with the media specialist taught me that true authenticity is being consistent with a message and that it is okay to internalize the important points of a particular topic. Understanding a few points at a significantly deep level allows you as a leader to stay focused on the important topics. If everything is important, nothing is important. When you are focused, you can stay on message. This not only helped me with the media, but it also helped me stay on message when communicating with students, the board, staff, and the community. I reminded myself that disciplined people, with disciplined thought, taking disciplined action get things done.

Hinojosa-ism

Disciplined people with disciplined thought take disciplined action and get things done.

Focused people are precise in thought and action.

Preparing ahead of time gave me the confidence and the tools to proactively establish relationships with the media for the long term and in the best interest of the school district. Being able to message important points to multiple audiences in a succinct manner has also benefited me personally and professionally. As a result, I developed a long-term media relations strategy that had a significant impact on the school districts I served, especially the Dallas Independent School District.

Media Roles Are Different

As a superintendent, you need to understand the mission and structure of each type of media organization. News stations, newspapers, journalists, and the like will all state that they are mission driven, and that their mission is to inform the public, especially about government. Despite what they may claim, almost all media organizations are profit driven first. The media must make money in order to accomplish their secondary mission. To remain independent, they cannot take tax dollars, which means that their sources of revenue are limited. Subscriptions are a small part of their revenue; the largest portion of their revenue comes from advertising dollars. Savvy superintendents understand this phenomenon and learn how to work with it.

With their senior team, a superintendent must develop relationships with each component of the various media outlets. Although online media and social media are growing in importance, print media still holds significant sway with voters. Thus, even though media and politics are distinct, they are also intertwined and influence each other in many ways. To navigate their connection successfully, superintendents must understand the structural differences among roles in the media. Knowing the difference between the motivation and goals of an investigative journalist versus a beat reporter will help you tailor your message based on who you are currently interacting with.

Key Players in Media

▶ *Editor:* a manager in charge of a specific area of the newspaper (digital or print); they filter and edit submissions.

▶ *Reporter:* the storyteller in front of the camera and the story chaser off camera, aggressively chasing leads and interviews.

▶ *Investigative reporter/journalist:* a type of reporter who performs extensive research and analysis to build facts and current events into news stories. They pursue leads, conduct interviews, and travel to different places to gather pieces of evidence and other source materials. They take videos or photographs and coordinate with experts when necessary.

▶ *Columnist:* a type of reporter who writes regularly for publication in a series, creating an article that usually offers commentary and opinions. They write with a specific point of view or voice. The column may appear in print or in digital format, such as a blog.

▶ *Beat reporter:* a reporter in charge of covering a specific story for an extended amount of time, such as neighborhood crime, school systems, or government accountability.

Hinojosa-ism

Say what you mean and mean what you say . . . but remember, people will pay more attention to what you do.

People do not believe what you say; they believe what you do. It is imperative to be clear and concise in communication.

During my time at Dallas ISD, I made it a priority to meet with the editorial board (typically a group of editors and sometimes writers and reporters) of the *Dallas Morning News* every quarter. In over a decade, I worked with various editors. The relationships were always professional but calculated depending on the status of the overall relationship. During that time, I had very close relationships with multiple members of the editorial board. They would call me occasionally on "background" to get further perspectives on big issues. They trusted me and I trusted them. This trust was built over time. I learned that there are two types of trust: technical trust and interpersonal trust. Technical trust is based upon competence. If a person is technically trustworthy, you can rely on the quality of their work. Interpersonal trust is built when confidential information is never betrayed. When the stakes are high, these types of relationships are critical.

Typically, at these quarterly meetings I would spend thirty minutes covering the three major initiatives we were working on as an administration. The remainder of the meeting time was spent on issues that the reporters wanted to probe further. Beat reporters would sit in on these meetings. This created a dicey situation on the two occasions when I made the mistake mentioning an issue that had not been fully baked with the school board.

In addition to working on my relationships with the editorial board, it was also very important to have good relationships with the beat reporters. Most minor issues were handled adequately and appropriately by our district's public information officer. The chief of communications, at times, handled elevated issues. But there were certain issues that only the superintendent could address. When a superintendent actively responds to beat reporters in a timely manner and with a positive approach, it fosters respect. So down the line, even if the reporter must report on a critical story, having the professional courtesy to grant access earns grace and helps ensure fairness. Superintendents who do not have professional relationships with beat reports seldom get the benefit of the doubt when a critical story gets published.

I have found investigative reporters to be a double-edged sword. In a nutshell, my advice for interacting with investigative reporters includes the following: You cannot ignore them, but you also cannot succumb blindly to their requests. Know their deadlines and empathize with their circumstances. Always be honest and never speculate. Acknowledge their questions and answer them directly if it is in the best interest of the district. If the issue jeopardizes the district in any significant way, block the question with an acknowledgment phrase and quickly bridge it to the important points. Here are a few examples:

▶ It is not quite that simple, but what is clear . . .

▶ That is not actually accurate, but what I assure you is . . .

▶ Before I tackle that, let me tell you what I do know . . .

▶ I don't have a crystal ball, but let me assure you that safety is our first priority.

▶ I have heard that, but let me bring clarity by . . .

Accessibility is critical, and not only for good news. Later in the chapter you will find a section on crisis communications and media relations. Superintendents gain credibility with the board, staff, and community when they handle difficult matters in the most transparent manner possible.

Lessons Learned: Working With the Media

▶ *Avoid taking cold calls.* Whether you are dealing with an editor, columnist, or reporter, if you take a cold call without at least some information on the topic, you could be caught in a difficult situation without an exit strategy.

▶ *Try to control who tells the story.* When you know a story is going to come out, it is better to occasionally tip a trusted reporter so that they get the lead on the story. Even if you know the story will reflect negatively on the district, it is better to tip a trustworthy person who will be as fair as possible.

▶ *Only embargo a story when you absolutely must.* Embargoing a story (the request/requirement by a source that the information provided not be published until a specific date or certain conditions have been met) should be saved for weighty issues that will have a significant impact on the school system, either in a positive or negative way.

> ## PRO TIP
>
> When you agree to give an interview, consider requesting that questions be emailed in advance so that you have time to craft thoughtful, informed, and accurate responses.

Media Relations With the School Board

Typically, school boards develop Board Operating Procedures. In most procedure manuals, the spokesperson for the board is the elected chair of the board. The spokesperson for the district is the superintendent, who will typically delegate minor issues to a key staff member. However, in large, urban districts many individual board members prefer not to give up the right to speak to the media directly. They may have a different point of view that they want to express. This can create significant tension among board members. As the superintendent, stay aware if this dynamic plays out with your school board so that you can navigate the personalities and issues around the differing perspectives with care.

It is best practice for the superintendent to keep the school board informed on a regular basis regarding all media contacts. No one likes surprises. For twenty-seven years, every Friday morning I sent a memo to the board, titled "Board Update." There was a section of the update that included all routine media contacts, with cursory information about the topic and individuals or schools involved.

In large, urban districts where the stakes are much higher, the media can be an ally in your work—for example in uncovering and addressing corruption. In my experience, many of the major corruption cases that the Federal Bureau of Investigations decides to pursue emanate from negative media stories. During my second tenure, I used information gleaned from a local television investigative reporter to take down a corrupt bus agency that had been providing transportation services to Dallas ISD for decades. Eventually the FBI and the courts sent five people to federal prison, including a local city councilman. Gaining the trust and respect of your local reporters can help you accomplish your goal of better serving students.

Media Relations During a Crisis

Media relations in a crisis are different from normal day-to-day media interactions. If you make a mistake or your staff makes a mistake, it is much better to own it and ask for forgiveness. Many criminals get convicted due to the coverup rather than the original crime. I learned the disarming power of admitting mistakes as a basketball referee when I admitted to a volatile coach that I missed a call. He forgave me because he knew he could trust me and requested me for his playoff games. The same is true with the media. If they know they can trust you, they give you grace. If you betray that confidence, then all bets are off.

Hinojosa-ism

You cannot talk your way out of things you behave your way into.

If you make a mistake, admit it. Most criminals get convicted for the coverup rather than the actual crime. Admitting mistakes is also very disarming.

When a crisis occurs, as the leader you must run to the problem, not away from it. Being accessible during a crisis is critical. If the leader refuses to be visible during the crisis, then the media immediately becomes suspicious. In my final years in Dallas, two major crises occurred that were out of my control: a tornado wiped out three schools in October 2019, followed in March 2020 by the COVID-19 pandemic. Immediately after the tornado I called a news conference and informed the entire community of the status of the damage and our plan to get over three thousand students into adequate learning environments within thirty-six hours. During the pandemic I scheduled regular news conferences to deliver status reports to the community via the media and addressed their questions, comments, and concerns.

Even though the superintendent is the CEO and responsible for the day-to-day operations of the district, it is always wise to call the school board chair at the beginning of any major crisis to seek guidance about how to communicate with the rest of the board. It is tempting to jump into problem-solving mode, which I have done before—much to my chagrin. As the head of one of the largest entities in the community, you are dealing with people's two most-prized possessions: their money and their children. They will have opinions for sure. You are operating in a politically charged environment, whether you choose to accept it or not. The sidebar on working with the media during a crisis shares some of the tenets I have learned over my many years of experience.

Lessons Learned: Working With the Media During a Crisis

▶ Never speculate. Ask for time to respond with facts when they become available.

▶ Have a consistent protocol for privacy matters such as legal, personnel, and student records. Always consult the Federal Education Records Privacy Act.

▶ If asked to comment on things that are not related to the district, avoid the temptation to do so.

▶ Confidence comes with having a plan. Here is a plan that has worked for me: Start with an opening statement, take limited questions, then acknowledge other questions and bridge to the important points in your message.

▶ Express empathy. You are ahead of the curve. You have been handling the crisis well ahead of everyone else, so you are naturally further through the emotional stages of dealing with change (shock, denial, anger/grief, acceptance). Remember to show empathy with others as they experience the news in real time.

The more time you spend in district leadership, the more you will see that some superintendents only deal with the media when delivering good news but let the communications department be the punching bag when delivering negative news. If you succumb to this strategy, you will lose credibility with the board, the staff, and the community. Great leaders accept the blame when things go wrong and give credit to everyone else when things go well.

> ## PRO TIP
>
> Great leaders accept the blame when things go wrong and give credit to everyone else when things go well.

Politics and Education

Politics, according to Wikipedia, can be defined as "the set of activities that are associated with making decisions in groups, or other forms of power relationships among those groups, such as the distribution of resources or status." Sounds innocuous enough, right? So why does politics get such a bad rap? It is because these days, partisan politics carries such negative energy, especially when driven by the extreme ends of the political spectrum.

Almost all major decisions are made in groups. What makes decision-making political is not necessarily the fact that a decision was made; it is more about the process behind the decision. Someone in the group had the most influence over that decision, but it is not always the person who has the most positional power. The most effective leaders may have authority but seldom use it. Leaders should always use their influence for the greater good, and sometimes that means letting someone else steer the ship (or at least think they are steering the ship) for a little while. Every group has people who play a variety of roles.

When considering the politics of running a school district, there is wisdom in remembering that your friends come and go but your enemies accumulate. Educational leaders must make difficult decisions in the best interest of their district, with the understanding that it may strain previously established relationships. Politics is about power and relationships and the art of compromise. Relationships are about influence. You may find that at some point, the people who you do not agree with are the ones you may need the most on an important issue. It is critical to never burn bridges, whether you win or lose on an issue. As distasteful as the word *politics* may be for you and may make you think about unsavory uses of power, I encourage you to quickly pivot to the word *influence* instead. Approaching politics as a way of using your influence for the ultimate benefit of the students you serve will help your psyche.

The Politics of Decision-Making

When making a decision of significant impact, consider three aspects of the proposed solution: (1) the legal answer, (2) the political answer, and (3) the practical answer. As a team, you first have to make sure that the solution is legal. But just because it is a legal course of action does not necessarily mean that it is a good solution. Next, ask the group if the solution would be a sound decision based on the politics involved. If you are lucky, the solution is legal, with limited political consequences. The third aspect of the solution to consider is practicality. If the decision is legal and politically viable, then what are the practical implications of the decision?

Consider, for example, a school board's proposal to significantly increase the tax rate to generate more revenue to fund the district's strategic initiatives. The school board may have the capacity to increase the tax rate by 5 cents, so the decision meets the first criteria, it is legal. The capacity exists to improve resources to accomplish the mission. However, when you consider the political ramifications of your decision you realize that three of your strongest supporters on the board are up for reelection at the same time as the tax increase would be on the ballot. Your supporters risk a high chance of being defeated in the election (those are high political implications!). However, the board decides to move forward with the tax increase and the three incumbent board members get defeated by three anti-tax candidates that pledge to the public to reduce taxes if elected. Instead of moving ahead with a legal decision that would not be politically expedient, you might consider a practical approach that would allow you to fund your initiative while retaining your key allies on the board. Novice superintendents often fail to consider all the dimensions of a problem before making recommendations on high-stakes decisions. To help guide problem-solving, consider using the decision tree in Figure 2.1.

All Politics Is Local

The saying "all politics is local" is particularly germane to school districts. While many people get excited with media coverage of international and national headlines, the fact remains that local

Figure 2.1 Considerations for High-Stakes Decision-Making

Decision/Situation Under Consideration			
Legal implications		No legal implications	
High political implications	Low political implications	High political implications	Low political implications
STOP	What's most practical?	STOP	What's most practical?

politics is what people care about the most. This phenomenon can partially be explained by the fact that school districts deal with matters that are important to most people. (Despite this fact, voter turnout for school board races is astonishingly low.)

People who benefited from the school system tend to want it to remain unchanged. Those tend to be the people with political clout in local systems. Even though I was not a great scholar, I loved school. I worked hard, and I never missed a day. Effort creates ability. But in the inner city of Dallas, I had classmates who were much smarter than me who were not benefiting from this version of school. Education needs to reinvent itself. Google changed the internet. Apple revolutionized the phone and computer industries. Uber turned the taxicab industry on its head. But nothing has revolutionized public education. Politics has a lot to do with this. Despite the calls for transformation and innovation, the power still rests with people who express the attitude, "It worked for me, therefore it should work for everybody." These are the people who tell educators how to do their jobs and they think their opinions are qualified simply because they attended schools.

Interacting With Government Entities and Elected Officials

As a former government teacher, I accepted that politics would be part of the job of being a superintendent. I have said many times that I understand politics, but I am not a politician. Many of my board members tell me that I am the best politician they know; I am just not an elected official. If I really think about it, being called a politician in this context is a compliment, according to the definition at the beginning of this section. It means that I have figured out how to effectively influence power relationships to benefit the school districts I have served. For the balance of the chapter, I will share what I have learned about what a superintendent needs to be aware of in dealing with governmental entities and elected officials.

Local Government

Interactions with elected officials beyond the school board are and will always be part of the job of the superintendent. The county or parish in which the school district is located can have a significant impact on school district operations. In some states the county has the taxing authority, and thus controls the purse strings. This dynamic creates the need for a close relationship between the superintendent and county authorities. In some states the county and the school district simply have the same boundaries, with little governance overlap. Even in states where significant independence from the county exists, there are some county departments that wield significant influence on school systems, such as the county health department as became obvious during the COVID-19 pandemic. Relationships with county elected officials that are developed consistently over time will pay off significantly when unforeseen situations occur.

Superintendents should have regularly scheduled meetings with the county executive regardless of whether the official is elected or appointed. In urban systems the namesake district is typically the largest district in the county. The power that the superintendent has should be used sparingly. Cooperation with other superintendents in the county will leverage win-win opportunities if utilized strategically.

Relationships with mayors are even more complex for various reasons. In districts where there is mayoral control, the directness of the relationship cannot be overstated. Instead of having multiple relationships with board members that need to be managed, this one relationship is crucial. In most instances there is significant alignment between the two individuals. One mayoral election could have a significant impact on this alignment. There have been instances when fallout occurs, and this could create a volatile situation for the superintendent.

In city districts where the school board hires the superintendent, it is imperative that the mayor and superintendent have a positive working relationship. In namesake cities, this is especially critical. This relationship should not be delegated to someone else on your staff. Maintaining these relationships can become complex when the superintendent serves several municipalities, each with its own mayor, as is often the case in metro areas. In most large cities, school board members take the initiative in establishing relationships with elected officials that have regional or district responsibilities and representation, such as city council members and county commissioners. While these relationships are delegated, the superintendent should never minimize the role of any elected official. Under no circumstances should a mayor ever feel disrespected by you or your office.

Many cities employ a city manager or chief executive officer of the city. It is extremely critical that a significant relationship exists between the city manager and superintendent. In my thirteen years as superintendent of Dallas, I had excellent relationships with three city managers. I convinced them to have quarterly meetings with our respective senior staff members. These sessions turned out to be extremely beneficial to each entity. (I will share more about these meetings in Chapter 4.)

Like county governance structures, city governance structures also vary significantly, depending on state and local laws, statutes, rules, ordinances, policies, and the like. Regardless of the structures, the superintendent needs to be comfortable building relationships with these external stakeholders to benefit the school district over the long haul. More detailed information about working with local government and community organizations will be shared in Chapter 4.

State Leadership and Legislation

Most superintendents underestimate the influence they can have on state legislators. This is especially true in the urban areas partly because of the impact politically savvy superintendents have on the media. Superintendents should nurture relationships with the local delegation of state representatives and senators in both political parties, regardless of their own personal political affiliation or beliefs. Urban superintendents who are willing to be engaged in the political process can also have significant influence on the state legislature as well, as they are de facto leaders in their states. Although some decline to take advantage of that situation, I chose to participate in every superintendent trade organization, both umbrella and niche organizations. I typically served as the legislative chair and eventually chair of each of these organizations. As a result, I had access to the ear of the state leadership (Governor, Lieutenant Governor, and Speaker of the House), even if we disagreed on partisan politics. I also had the opportunity to be at the table when major decisions were made. I strongly believe that militants never get to the table, and, if by chance they get there, they do not get to stay. I was either the legislative chair or president of the following organizations: Texas Association of School Administrators, Texas School Alliance, Texas Urban Council, and Fast Growth Coalition of Schools. My direct and consistent involvement at the state level benefited the districts that I served.

During my tenure, I often heard Texas legislators complain that school superintendents were against everything and for nothing. That was not productive, so a group of us within the Texas Association of School Administrators (TASA) organized a visioning institute (funded through TASA) to define and articulate the causes we advocated. That approach proved to be more effective. We worked together for nine months to create a document outlining our goals. It led to some innovation, but unfortunately it did not transform public education as much as we had hoped. I threatened to leave the group because it was not *bold* enough; there was too much incrementalism. However, I am glad I participated because it helped me in the next decade to transform Dallas ISD—with a lot help from others.

In working with registered lobbyists, a group of savvy superintendents and I figured out how and when to play defense versus offense and vice versa. We learned that it was much easier to kill bills rather than to pass bills. We figured out how the timelines worked by playing delay games and implementing procedural tactics to allow politicians to claim victory by having a bill pass in committee but die in the calendar process. Politically savvy superintendents develop relationships with staffers of key legislators, many of whom are very young and inexperienced but wield significant influence with their bosses.

Many legislative leaders figured out how to get to the matter of motivation. Some legislation that was unpopular with many stakeholders was passed by incentivizing the behavior they desired.

They would make the legislation voluntary, then provide significant resources if stakeholders participated in the project. The legislation was not an unfunded mandate, it was now a funded incentive. This was a great example of the definition of politics previously articulated. Groups that were making big decisions found a way to study the power relationships in other key groups they needed to generate enough support to get ownership from key stakeholders. Here are some strategic moves that all superintendents should understand to help pick battles wisely and become politically savvy:

Strategic Political Moves for the Savvy Superintendent

▶ **Understand that politics makes for strange bedfellows.**
People who seldom agree can sometimes find a key issue on which they agree. Power relationships are critical to making things happen for the greater good. Unfortunately, these same power relationships can coalesce for evil. Understand that this phenomenon can work both ways.

▶ **Study power relationships for the purpose of identifying mutual benefits.**
You have more in common with your enemy than you may think. With an open mind and hard work, you will discover shared values, beliefs, and issues that can bring people together for the common good. There are people who might dislike each other but have similar personality styles that allow them to relate to each other on specific topics. Power mapping is an organized method that can benefit a group of diverse leaders. By knowing as much as possible about the people you interface with, you'll be better able to create conditions for people to seek meaningful solutions with mutual benefits.

▶ **Believe in the power of building guiding coalitions.** Transformations fail because guiding coalitions to solve big problems rarely exist. Your job is to negotiate good faith commitments from diverse stakeholders who have a bona fide mutual interest in the outcome or solution. Getting stakeholders to adopt the

(Continued)

(Continued)

definition of consensus as "not your way or my way, but a better way" will create the conditions for compromise. These conditions can be created so that the coalition can flourish in the best interest of all stakeholders, particularly the students. Win-win deals are possible, but if and only if there is a genuine willingness and ability to compromise.

The Big Ideas

Being a successful superintendent means navigating the world of media and politics. Here are the big ideas I shared in Chapter 2:

 Be authentic and stay focused on your message.
Understanding a few points at a significantly deep level allows you as a leader to stay focused on the important topics. If everything is important, nothing is important.

 Build relationships with a variety of people in the media.
There are many different roles and media outlets that you should be familiar with. Having trust and accessibility is key with the media, as you never know when the circumstances will arise (positive or negative) that you will need to be able to leverage or depend on those relationships.

 Confidence with media and politics comes with time and experience.
The more people you meet, the more experiences you have, and the more conversations you are a part of, the more comfortable and confident you will become. What is most important is to always stay in the conversation rather than shy away from it.

 Politics is part of the role of superintendent whether you like it or not.
Whether it's getting something passed with the school board, putting a new bond measure up for consideration in your city, or simply having a conversation with a local reporter or city

councilperson, politics is always at play. Make that reality work to the advantage of your school district and the students, educators, and families you serve.

▶ **Know who votes.**

Voting blocs in school systems are typically stable, but from time to time the people who do not agree with each other may vote together on an issue. Elections can and will impact your success. You are not a politician or elected official, but you are a public official. School board elections have the lowest voter turnout of most forms of government. Disaggregation of who votes must be analyzed and contemplated. During my tenure in Dallas, the most common voter was White women over sixty. The next voting bloc was White men, followed closely by Black women. Black men and Latinos were the lowest percentage of voters. Voters determine who the employer of the superintendent will be and the type of resources (via referendums) that will be available for the school district.

CHAPTER #2

Reflect and Act

Now it's time to reflect on what you've read and decide how you can best apply the insights gained from the chapter in practical ways within your district. Use this modified "five 'A's" protocol (Agree, Argue, Apply, Actions, and Accountable) to journal your ideas.

What do you **agree** with in the chapter?	What do you want to **argue** about within the chapter?
How can you **apply** the information from this chapter to your own district?	What **actions** can you take after reading this chapter? And how will you hold yourself **accountable**?

Adapted from Judith Gray, "Four 'A's Text Protocol," National School Reform Faculty (2005), www.nsrfharmony.org.

CHAPTER 3

Nurture Excellence in Your Staff

Typically, human capital makes up approximately 80 percent of a school district budget. Building the right kind of systems, processes, and protocols is critical for a superintendent to be able to manage a significant portion of the resources available to lead. Also, a key to success is careful planning of strategy when guiding a large, complex governmental entity that has many stakeholders, especially the public.

Labor Relations for Positive District Climate and Staff Retention

Part of creating a culture and climate that leads to student success is working with the labor or union organizations in your district or state. I served in two different states as a superintendent. Both states, Texas and Georgia, are known as right-to-work states; therefore, I never had to engage in collective bargaining over teacher contracts with any local union organizations. However, often teachers would choose to belong to national union organizations, such as the American Federation of Teachers (AFT). I was a member of AFT during my teaching career.

As superintendent, I worked very effectively with the AFT in Dallas. The local affiliate is known as the Alliance. While we occasionally disagreed on philosophy and some significant issues such as pay for performance for teachers, we had a healthy respect for each other, which allowed us to work well together in support of teachers. One way I did this was through strategic representation.

The Texas Education Code requires every district to have a committee known as the District Education Improvement Council. Teachers, principals, parents, and community members are required to be represented on the council. I regularly appointed leaders of both local affiliates (the American Federation of Teachers and the National Education Association) to serve on this group. I appointed non-organization teachers as well, but I felt it was important to include the teacher organizations to help ensure that all perspectives were represented within the council.

In right-to-work states, teacher organizations do not have collective bargaining contracts; however, they do have a say at the ballot box. In certain communities and urban areas, unions can have a significant impact on school board elections, where voter turnout tends to be low. In states that do have collective bargaining and union contracts, this creates challenges for school districts, especially those that want to execute transformational ideas. Superintendents need to understand the land-scape of labor relations and collective bargaining to effectively navigate the waters. In my opinion, the person who did this most effectively was Dr. Joe Gothard, the former superintendent of the Saint Paul Public Schools, in Minnesota. I asked Dr. Gothard to share a high-level over-view of his key strategies for success. This is what he had to say.

Setting the Table: What I Learned While Managing Teacher Contract Collective Bargaining

by Joe Gothard

I began my tenure as the superintendent of Saint Paul Public Schools (SPPS) on July 1, 2017. My career in education has taken me to three school districts, each with strong histories of collective bargaining. While I was building relationships with new stake-holders in SPPS, I made sure that the leader of the teachers' union was one of the people I connected with early on. During that summer meeting, a packet of contract proposals was shared with me to begin my negotiations with the St. Paul Federation of Teachers (the union added the Education Support Professionals and School and Community Service Professionals in 2019 and changed their name to the Saint Paul Federation of Educators, SPFE). It is also important to note that at the present time SPPS has 27 unique bargaining groups.

Prior to beginning bargaining sessions, I knew that I had to share my expectations for how the administration was organized for contract negotiations. I convened our board of education in legally noticed closed sessions to begin our strategy work.

Setting the direction with our board of education included these steps:

▶ **Create a set of guiding principles and negotiation priorities.** Guiding principles were developed to identify key strategic elements and behaviors that the administration was committed to. Negotiation priorities listed the top two or three goals of negotiations. As an example, in the 2017 negotiations, raising

(Continued)

(Continued)

the minimum wage to $15 per hour was a priority. The list of principles and priorities were shared publicly and presented to all SPPS bargaining groups.

▶ **Set a financial pattern for all bargaining groups.**
Once the board received a presentation on district finances, the administration recommended an overall dollar percentage increase to be invested in the cost of the contract. The financial parameters were shared publicly for the bargaining groups and district stakeholders.

My experiences in SPPS quickly taught me the importance of understanding the bargaining process and the history. I led our administration four times during my nearly 7-year tenure in SPPS in bargaining with SPFE. Each session was emotional, drawn out, and contentious. For greater context, here is a list of the key developments in each of those contract cycles:

2017–2019 Contract: Joint file for mediation, union strike authorization, letter of intent to strike, contract settled during 10-day cooling off, and strike averted.

2019–2021 Contract: Union file for mediation, union strike authorization, letter of intent to strike, 5-day strike.

2021–2023 Contract: Union file for mediation, union strike authorization, letter of intent to strike, contract settled in final hours of 10-day cooling off period, and strike averted.

2023–2025 Contract: Joint file for mediation, union strike authorization, letter of intent to strike, contract settled during 10-day cooling off period, and strike averted.

The recent labor movement in public education reaches deep into communities, engaging passionate stakeholders. Consistently throughout my four cycles of bargaining with our teachers' union, their successful organizing created a polarization that made it extremely difficult to maintain our guiding principles, priorities, and financial parameters.

(Continued)

"Remember, when it comes to community organizing the goal is to attack people, not a process. Processes don't have feelings or families."

—Joe Gothard, 2023

Community organizing can result in polarization between labor groups and management. Both sides are charged with creating positive outcomes and experiences for students. It is important to maintain collaborative relationships even when put through the test of contentious contract negotiations. Below are some helpful steps to consider when negotiating labor contracts.

▶ **Plan Communications Thoughtfully**
Create a detailed plan to manage all information related to contract negotiations. Articulate with your leadership team and board of directors what information is public and private. Establish a cadence of written updates to all district staff and families. Be prepared to send messages if things escalate and the union begins to organize with public testimony, press conferences, and email campaigns, to name a few tactics. Should things escalate to the threat of a strike, a strike planning team should be created and the community must be aware what district leadership is planning in the event of a work stoppage. Finally, once a settlement is reached, manage the emotion of the moment and fall back on the guiding principles and priorities that you established with the board of education.

▶ **Familiarize Yourself With the History of Superintendent and Board of Education Roles in Previous Negotiations**
As a rule, the district will likely have a history for how it has engaged with the teachers' union for negotiations. Being clear with all parties is important to avoid potential conflicts. The use of closed sessions with the board as permitted by law is important for continued information sharing and strategic guidance. As negotiations get closer to a potential settlement, there might be room to hold the board in closed session at or

(Continued)

(Continued)

near the site of negotiations. As negotiations begin to move quickly and you are relying on board guidance, the timing of being able to swiftly address differences between the two parties is a priority. There may be pressure for board members and/or the superintendent to be present at negotiations. Those decisions should be made jointly. However, once the board or the superintendent shows up, they must remain for the duration of the negotiations.

Know Your Stakeholders

People on all sides of contract negotiations deeply admire the people involved; but they might despise the situation. There will be allegations of erroneous budget information, historical promises that were made and not kept will be revealed, and today more than ever students may even join in organizing alongside their teachers. The teachers' union and community will plead for transparency and the polarity of messages will undoubtedly create questions of who to believe. There may also be times where the board may be split on the strategy or potential resolutions. Remember, when conducting press conferences or online messaging to the public, you are speaking to staff, parents, and students. The opportunity to educate your closest stakeholders should not be taken lightly.

All *Things* Communication

As the pressure continues to mount on the negotiations team, it is important to note that the team reports to the superintendent. Their communication (spoken and written) *is* the superintendent's voice. The guiding principles are a great tool for superintendents to constantly draw upon in leading their teams. Expect your personal and work social media accounts to be weaponized. Our team in SPPS created a website dedicated to contract negotiations. We collected all information shared so that it could be stored and easy to find. This includes updates to staff and families, videos and press conferences, budget information, and the actual open negotiations proposals from both the teachers' union and the district. Finally, find a good rhythm to over-communicate to the board. Eliminate surprises and assist the board of education in managing the emotions of negotiations. Remember that individual board members may have been

(Continued)

endorsed by union members who also might have assisted in their election campaigns to the school board.

▌ **Manage Your Team's Emotions—Not Their Jobs**
Begin team planning sessions with updates. Let your team know what you are hearing from the board, from email communication received, and from local political officials. Keeping those responsible for negotiations in the loop builds trust and confidence. Keep a close eye on the number of hours being spent at the table and in planning for negotiations. Keep your team fresh by allowing flex time on calendars, especially when they are committed to consecutive days of bargaining. One of the most important lessons I've learned is that although I've had different levels of involvement in negotiations during my tenure at SPPS based on a number of factors, I always had a say in who was part of the negotiations team. The team charged with planning and presenting at the table during bargaining is critically important. Even one member of the team who is not respected or brings negative energy can have a consequential impact on the overall success of the team and ultimately the ability to settle the contract. Superintendents must monitor the emotion of the room and be prepared to address conflict early in the process.

▌ **Clearly Understand and Help Define Board Expectations of the Superintendent**
Recognize that there may likely be board of education division regarding how to successfully negotiate a teacher contract settlement. It might be over the amount of financial investment, it could be for staffing levels, and it could even be the slightest language item that is personally meaningful to a board member. As the leader, it is important to focus on tasks and not the drama of the moment. If available, ensure that your General Counsel is available for all closed sessions. Especially if the negotiations are headed toward the path of work stoppage, your General Counsel is a trusted advisor to both the administration and the school board.

These examples are a small sample of what I've learned in four contract negotiations cycles with the teacher's union in Saint Paul

(Continued)

(Continued)

Public Schools. Some of the greatest challenges I've faced as a superintendent have also turned into the greatest leadership learning. If you are considering becoming a superintendent in a school district that engages in collective bargaining, it is important to learn about the history of that district and how it might impact your ability to be successful as a leader.

Hinojosa-ism

Discussion means let me convince you that I am right. Dialogue means that it is not your way and not my way, but a better way.

Rigid people who do not believe in the art of compromise try to bully others to get their way. True dialogue is trying to find the best way.

Train and Retain High-Quality Educators and Staff

When I was a teacher, an assistant principal tapped me on the shoulder and insisted that I go back to school to get my master's degree. I told him that I wanted to coach all my life, but their insistence pushed me out of my comfort zone to try something new. That scenario repeated itself for the rest of my career—someone tapped me on the shoulder and pushed me forward. With a significant degree of intentionality, I chose to give back to potential leaders by identifying them, developing them, and helping them get promoted. Many do not realize what talents they possess until someone points it out to them and then does something about it.

Ultimately, the superintendent must be the owner of training and retaining staff because it impacts culture. You can delegate almost everything, but one thing that should never be delegated is culture and climate. The superintendent must model this core belief by becoming the head coach. The abundance mentality is critical in this case. There are three distinct steps to building a culture of staff excellence:

1. Identify talent and potential
2. Develop skills and pave the path to promotion
3. Promote people with proven skills and potential

Throughout this chapter, I share how I work with key chiefs to help me use this three-step process with three separate groups of people: the Executive Leadership Team, the Principal Group, and the HiPo Group.

PRO TIP

Be the owner of training and retaining staff. One thing that should never be delegated is culture and climate. The superintendent must model this core belief by becoming the head coach.

Identify Talent and Potential

At the beginning of their tenure, every superintendent must have an entry plan. Most superintendent development and preparation organizations teach a very prescriptive entry plan that is pre-ordained and rigid. The entry plan that I described in Chapter 1 is organic and dynamic. My entry plan asks 100 people 10 questions. Question number 4 is always, "Who are the most respected people on staff?" The feedback is typically direct and specific. By following this process, talent can be identified at the inception. Once the report becomes public, it will be obvious how to proceed with the talent you have identified.

The Executive Leadership Team (ELT)

Once every six months I meet with the key chiefs to identify the best principal in the district. Multiple data sets are used, such as absolute student performance, value-added achievement, and culture and climate on the campus. Once that person is identified, they are given a temporary six-month seat on the Executive Leadership Team. (I will share more about that team in the next section, on talent development.) This process is repeated every six months. In my career, almost fifty leaders who have worked with me have become super-intendents, and at least half of those started as a principal on the ELT.

The Principal Group

Once per year the same chiefs meet with me to review similar data to identify the top fifteen principals. The caveat is that the fifteen must be diverse in every sense of the word. Diversity in race, ethnicity, gender, campus type and level, etc. Over the next school year, these fifteen principals form the Principal Group. I describe what they do in the talent development section.

The HiPo Group

HiPo is short for high-potential—employees who must be developed. Once per year I meet with my senior staff and follow the Nominal Group Technique process to identify central office employees who exhibit the most potential. Each chief gets to nominate up to three individuals in their division who exhibit significant talent and high potential. The process uses a weighted voting formula that identifies the top fifteen employees who become part of the HiPo Group. In the talent development section, I describe what the HiPo Group does.

The Nominal Group Technique

This is a group brainstorming strategy where everyone writes down their ideas or solutions about an issue, problem, or challenge. Then each group member presents their favorite idea, and all suggestions are discussed, ranked, and prioritized. This strategy provides an opportunity for everyone's ideas and opinions to be taken into consideration.

For twenty-seven years, I met with my direct reports on a quarterly basis. They had to execute a one-page document that asked five questions. They would submit the document the day before the session. I stole this idea from management guru Tom Peters. He called it To Resume. I kept the name. Questions 1, 2, 4, and 5 varied and were about strategic initiatives, professional growth, random projects that were important to the district, SMART goals for their division, and a myriad of other topics. Question 3 was always about relationships that are key. The most typical question was, "In the last six months, who did you rely on the most to get your work done?"

I wrote down the names of the people whose names came up most often and made it a point to start following the work of those employees in an informal manner. This helped not only in talent identification but would later pay huge dividends when it came to succession planning.

Talent identification is a critical attitude or disposition that a successful superintendent must have. Identification by itself is useless unless you do something with it. That something is development and promotion, which are the next two sections of this chapter.

Develop Skills and Pave the Path to Promotion

Talent management must be an attitude. That is why I visited schools unannounced every Wednesday for twenty-seven years. People would ask me why I visited schools so often. My response was, "Because that is where the talent is—both students and staff!" Then I would immediately be asked, "Why Wednesdays?" My response was, "Why not?!" I did not go to schools to "snoopervise"; I am an optimistic person. The middle of the week always seemed like a good time to see people at their best.

My school visits were very organized and routine. I would drive around the school to look at the grounds and the general conditions of the physical building. I did this because in my district, like many others around the country, most people who live near the schools do not have children in the building, but they pay taxes to support public education. These taxpayers care about the appearance of the buildings. Before I got out of the car, I would pull out my tablet to review all the data about the school so that I was prepared when I talked to the principal, staff, or any students.

I would check in with the school secretary, because we all know who really runs the school. I would ask the principal to walk me around the campus. I would ask to meet the custodian on duty. If the school was clean, I would praise the custodian. If not, I would just be cordial and never criticize. I then would go to the cafeteria and wave at the staff. In later years, they wanted to stop working and take selfies with me. I was quite embarrassed at the recognition, but part of the job is being visible and building relationships. Then I would walk every hallway, peeking into the classrooms without interrupting instruction. I asked the principal three to five open-ended questions like, "What are your demographics, major challenges, and what are you most proud of?" The questions were not important; it was really the answers that were important. If they complained about the parents or did not know their academic data, then we had a problem.

I only gave praise and never embarrassed anyone. But I noticed everything. My chief of schools and maintenance departments would be on pins and needles every Wednesday morning. If I saw a problem, I would let them know and give them the opportunity to resolve the matter if possible. I ignored nothing. If the problems were minor, we would discuss them later at a routine staff meeting. Only twice in twenty-seven years did a significant staffing change need to be made because of a visit.

Hinojosa-ism

Don't steal people's dignity.

Praise in public and reprimand in private. People will never forgive you if you publicly take their dignity.

When I was a human resources executive in Grand Prairie, I learned about the power of the Gallup Organization's research on teacher selection. They utilized a tool called Selection Research Incorporated, or SRI. When I first became a superintendent, I was the final interview of all employees. Both Fabens ISD and Region 19 Education Service Center were very small organizations. I approved over 95 percent of the recommendations. For my entire career I was the final interviewer for all principals, regardless of the size of the district. Hays Consolidated Independent School District was the last district where I interviewed teachers, all teachers. Talent management in a labor-intensive organization is paramount. While these examples are generic and help identify and potentially develop leaders, there must be a strategy to get better results.

The Executive Leadership Team

Having a principal on the ELT is a trick of the trade that I borrowed from a superintendent who I respected. His design was very different. He had one of his best friends, who was a golfing buddy, serve on his senior team. He was one of the two high school principals, and he was a permanent member of the team. I took the idea and made it a six-month term. It gave me a chance to get to know principals in a more intimate manner. My chiefs also benefited in the same way. It also gave more individuals the opportunity to get a significant peek at how the district worked beyond their campuses.

My ELT meetings were for important but not urgent matters. They were scheduled for 8:37 a.m. every other Monday morning. They lasted for approximately three hours, and I facilitated each session. In a Tom Peters's book called *The Tom Peters Seminar: Crazy Times Call for Crazy Organizations*, he pointed out that no one will forget an odd start time. I have a rigorous relationship with time. I tell my staff, "If you are early, you are late." Everyone would be in the room by 8:30 a.m., engaging in small talk. At 8:37 a.m. sharp, I started the meeting. Every time a new principal joined the team or when we had visitors, I would go over the simple ground rules.

> We start on time and finish on time.

> What is said in here stays in here, no attribution.

> What is learned here, leaves here.

> Take care of yourself, there are no breaks.

> It is okay to have fun.

There was always a written agenda, and any team member could put an item on the agenda. The agenda item was due to my secretary by noon the Wednesday before the Monday meeting. Any attachments were due by noon on Thursday. By noon on Friday, my secretary would distribute the agenda to the entire team. All ELT members had the weekend to review the agenda so that they could be prepared to have a dialogue once the meeting started. The decks were limited to ten slides, however some members got creative by including an appendix. That strategy eventually ended when people got carried away. Agenda items had to be important matters that typically impacted multiple divisions and possibly the entire district. There was another meeting for urgent matters.

This experience allowed principals to broaden their perspectives about leadership, the district, and themselves. They also became champions for the district as they understood the reasons for some of the major decisions made by the administration. When divisions such as finance, operations, communication, human capital, research, and curriculum brought important items to the table, their development exploded. At the end of the six months a retreat would be scheduled off-site for a day and a half to do future planning. In the later years, the retreats were hosted at my residence.

Some principals engaged more than others, but all were appreciative of the opportunity. In districts with over 100,000 students, I added the best principal supervisor to the rotation, thus expanding the development of more leaders and extending the circle of influence for all. These leaders became advocates for the district. Most of them started seeking and earning promotions creating win/win opportunities for all concerned.

The Principal Group

Each year, I took this group through a rigorous development initiative that lasted the entire year. My chief of staff and I met with them six times per year for half-day sessions. All these sessions were at pristine off-site locations, many of which were donated by industry partners. Diversity was an important component of the structure and design of the program. The group consisted of male, female, Latino, Black, and White principals. They represented elementary, middle, and high schools. Included were comprehensive neighborhood schools and specialty schools, such as magnet and choice schools. Performance and diversity were key selection criteria for the program.

It was stressed at the beginning of each cohort that the participants would learn significantly from the curriculum. I intended to teach them any and everything I knew about leadership and strategy. But I also stressed that they would learn from each other. I emphasized the power of the cohort. They would learn not only from my chief of staff and me but also from the talents each would bring to the group.

Over the years the agenda changed, but there were key components that were consistent. Each of the participants were required to make best practices presentations to the cohort. They got to choose what they were best in class at and share with the team members. Many participants formed relationships that would benefit them for the balance of their careers as they would clearly articulate for years.

The primary purpose of the Principal Group was to create a professional learning community that would serve as a think tank for the superintendent. The group provided input on matters that impacted student achievement, feedback on district initiatives, and a significant professional learning experience. Due to my optimistic perspective, the group allowed me to spend significant time with the best and most successful principals. I chose to focus on strengths.

During the first session I focused on leadership. I did an activity that had them identify the traits of the most inspiring leaders they had ever known or admired. The group came up with the adjectives that described these tremendous leaders. They were categorized into three groups: knowledge, skills, and attitudes. Invariably, everyone concluded that a super majority of the traits were attitudes.

At the same session, I led an activity to teach each of them how to identify, appreciate, and support all personality styles in any group. I shared instances in which understanding and modeling acceptance of all styles would pay significant dividends in their roles as leaders. Understanding and appreciating the various personalities, leadership, and learning styles invariably led to high-performing teams. One of my strongest skill sets is team building.

The Principal Group members were given the opportunity to shadow me in various activities. They could choose from the following activities: attend a meeting of one of my leadership teams, tag along on a school visit, or attend a community advisory committee meeting. Later they were given the opportunity to share with the group their observations from the shadowing experience. One of the latter sessions was devoted to a matter of significance that the group wanted to take a deeper dive into. The topics ranged from the district's Theory of Action, a bond election, strategic initiatives, the response to the pandemic, and the like.

Developing Talent Is Never a Waste of Time

Someone once asked me why I would develop talent in a person who might leave and work elsewhere. My response was that they would be serving children somewhere, and we never know who will come back to us and serve in leadership roles. We should always take the opportunity to help develop people's talents and strengths.

The HiPo Group

The development of this group mirrored the Principal Group protocols. The results were the same: outstanding! I had the opportunity to directly develop about fifteen key central office leaders every year for five years. I learned as much from these seventy-five leaders as they did from me.

Hinojosa-ism

You can fire them, or you can fire them up.

A principal once told me that he had to fire all his teachers because most of them were burned out. I said, "At least they were once lit."

Promote People With Proven Skills and Potential

My optimistic belief in people gives me a competitive advantage over superintendents who are less optimistic. In my career as superintendent of six different educational systems, I have never taken any executive staff member with me to a new position. In Dallas I did hire two executives twice, but in different terms. I believe that I have the knowledge, skills, and attitude to find and develop the talent in the system. At certain stages in my career, I led organizations that had not yet developed the talent in a few key areas. There were times in my career that external hires were needed, critical, and appropriate. After the CEO has had the opportunity to develop talent, external hires should be the exception not the norm.

Grow Your Pipeline

Public education is in the teaching and learning business. This should apply to the adults as well as the students. In Dallas ISD, we used to have to go to Mexico, Puerto Rico, and Spain to recruit teachers. Now we go to Oak Cliff and Pleasant Grove, two inner-city communities in Dallas that are now producing talented educators thanks to our "grow your own" pipeline in partnership with local universities.

It took me years to figure out that internal hires were superior to hiring from outside the system. Initially, I felt that it was important to import talent. I still do, but only in specific circumstances. There was a degree of flattery in selecting people who wanted to be part of our system. It was not until I understood the power of climate and culture that I learned to appreciate the internal hire mystique. Employees from the outside must learn the job and the district. It also sends a message to internal staff members about how much they are valued.

Talent promotion is critical at all levels. Students who become teachers in their local districts have more skin in the game than those who do not. Talented teachers need to see upward mobility if they are interested in leaving the classroom. Educator pipelines are extremely critical for the long-term success of school districts. Some teachers do not want to become administrators but have upward mobility as instructional coaches or other central staff support positions. Virtually all principals and assistant principals were teachers.

People who aspire to be career assistant principals should be avoided. If the leader believes in talent management defined with the components of identifying, developing, and promoting talented people, then career assistant principals clog the pipeline. Typically, most school districts have programs to develop future principals. Dallas ISD had a robust program called Leader Excellence, Advancement, and Development (LEAD). In my later years the program produced outstanding candidates. Elementary principalships were typically not difficult to fill. There were numerous outstanding candidates to select from for elementary schools and specialty schools (magnet and choice). Middle schools were much more difficult to fill, and it was not unusual to only have one excellent candidate for a high school. In fact, in my last year as a superintendent, the district created a position called "principal in residence," who would shadow an outstanding high school principal for a year. This was a position above the normal staffing formulas and was a classic supply-and-demand solution for an area of great need.

Over time, I learned a strategy that avoided employment mistakes. When there was a key vacancy at a campus or district and there was not an obvious choice to fill the position, I implemented a temporary solution. I hired either an Interim [position title] or an Acting [position title]. I used the term "interim" to signify to everyone that the employee in the position would not be a candidate for the permanent job and in fact was just holding the position until a permanent replacement could be identified. I used the term "acting" to signify that the employee in the position was auditioning for the job, and the expectation was that they would eventually earn the permanent title. Most of the time they did earn the job, but not always. This strategy solved a lot of hiring headaches.

Public education is labor intensive. Having a talent management strategy and plan is vital to every superintendent. This is non-negotiable to ensure that students benefit in the long run. The strategy must have multiple facets in the identification of talented employees, the development of these staff members, and the opportunity for promotion of these individuals.

The processes utilized in any system are important. The systems and details are paramount. They must be intentional and precise. The power lies in the CEO (the superintendent) of the system who models the execution of the talent management system. Culture and climate cannot be delegated. Talent management is a huge lever in improving culture and climate in a complex system such as a school district.

PRO TIP

Have a talent management strategy. The strategy must identify talented employees, plan for their professional development, and include a structure for their promotion.

Sustain Momentum: Passing the Torch

Great organizations engage in succession planning to ensure the long-term success of the district. Officially, you cannot select your replacement because that decision rests with the school board. However, if things are going well in the district when the superintendent vacates the position the school board will first look to internal candidates. If things are not going well or if there are no internal candidates prepared for the job, then the board must consider external candidates.

When I left Dallas the first time, I was not planning to leave. I got a great opportunity in Cobb County, Georgia, and I felt that I left Dallas high and dry. Cobb County had failed their search in 2011 and the board directed their attorney to find out who the best superintendents in the country were. When their attorney called and asked if I was interested, I did not even know where Cobb County was. He said that Cobb was a great district but had two major problems: they had a fractured board and the local newspaper was brutal on the district.

During my superintendency in Cobb County, we settled the board down and developed a relationship with the media. I also began grooming the head of technology as my successor, as he was well respected even though he was not a traditional educator. The board was appreciative and selected him as interim superintendent when I left. He went on to serve as superintendent for more than a decade.

When I returned to Dallas, I immediately began thinking about my succession plan. I knew I would retire eventually, and I did not want to leave the district high and dry again. I wanted them to be able to continue the momentum I knew we would be making. So, I required the chief of every major division (staff, school leadership, teaching and learning, operations, finance, technology, human capital, technology, and communications) to hire two deputy chiefs so that the district would have multiple highly effective leaders ready to step into positions as vacancies occurred. If at least one of them was ready, we appointed them as chief. If neither one was quite ready, we would appoint one of them as acting chief so they could audition for the post. If neither were close to being ready, we would appoint an interim chief who would not be a candidate but would hold the position until we found a permanent replacement. The plan worked. Talented executives were promoted swiftly as vacancies occurred. Dallas ISD was like Alabama football—we did not rebuild, we reloaded.

Developing Talent

One of my proudest accomplishments is that forty-five people who have worked with me have become chief executive officers of educational institutions. The group is very diverse:

▶ 32 males, 13 females

▶ 19 Latino, 18 White, 7 Black, 1 other

▶ They have worked in Texas, Georgia, Maryland, New Mexico, Arizona, Wisconsin, and Colorado

During my last two years in the Dallas ISD, I created a new deputy superintendent position. I advertised the position nationally.

My chief of school leadership would have been a logical successor, but they took a position elsewhere as superintendent in a major urban district. Up until this time, the chief of school leadership and the chief of teaching and learning had always reported directly to me. We interviewed three successful sitting superintendents from throughout the country, and I selected one of them as deputy superintendent.

I reorganized the central office so that only the chief of staff and two deputy superintendents reported to me directly. One deputy superintendent was responsible for finance, operations, and technology. The succession plan deputy superintendent for leading and learning was responsible for school leadership, teaching and learning, and human capital. The chief of staff had all other divisions, including communications. The two deputies and the chief of staff were appointed as trustee liaisons to the board members. The succession liaison was assigned to the board president and started assuming many duties, such as agenda planning. The succession deputy was assigned leadership roles in each corner of the Success Triangle.

When I announced my retirement, it was assumed by most of the staff and community that the succession deputy would be appointed as my replacement. I have said many times that you should never predict what a school board will do, as you will often be wrong. They ended up doing a national search and selected the former chief of schools who had been a superintendent for almost two years in another major district in Texas. Even though the school board didn't select an internal candidate, the one selected had worked as my chief of school leadership for five years; I felt comfortable that my succession plan had worked to a significant degree. The new superintendent was surrounded by knowledgeable and extremely capable chiefs from day one. Good things happen by design, not by accident.

The Big Ideas

Being a successful superintendent means training and retaining high-quality educators and staff. Here are the big ideas shared in Chapter 3:

> ▸ **Labor relations is a challenging reality of the job.**
> Unless you are a superintendent in a right-to-work state, negotiating labor contracts is a necessary aspect of your

position. Clear communication and planning are essential for success.

▶ **Action is important.**
Talent identification is important. You must know who the talented people are in the system. Once you know who they are, take time to develop them into better leaders. But none of that matters if you do not promote those leaders into key positions in the future.

▶ **Cultivate leadership within your organization.**
Form strategic groups (e.g., the Principal Group or HiPo) to build leadership skills within the employees you already have. In the long run, your organization will function more smoothly, and your students will benefit from continuity of leadership.

▶ **Keep the best in order to be the best.**
By providing educators and staff with opportunities to learn and grow, you provide a sense of family and belonging where they want to stay and where they feel valued in the long term.

▶ **Plan for the future.**
Even if you are early in your career, you will not be around forever. Think ahead about which systems, supports, and people you can put in place that will enable your district to keep the momentum going even after you leave.

Reflect and Act

Now it's time to reflect on what you've read and decide how you can best apply the insights gained from the chapter in practical ways within your district. Use this modified "five 'A's" protocol (Agree, Argue, Apply, Actions, and Accountable) to journal your ideas.

What do you **agree** with in the chapter?	What do you want to **argue** about within the chapter?
How can you **apply** the information from this chapter to your own district?	What **actions** can you take after reading this chapter? And how will you hold yourself **accountable**?

Adapted from Judith Gray, "Four 'A's Text Protocol," National School Reform Faculty (2005), www.nsrfharmony.org.

CHAPTER 4

Build Community Relations and Transparent Performance Management Systems

Most people might assume that community relations and a superintendent's performance management strategy would be two distinct initiatives. However, I learned (especially in Dallas) that combining these two dissimilar foci resulted in a powerful transformation of a school system that the mainstream community had given up on. Arguably, Dallas ISD is now one of the best and highest-performing urban school districts in the United States. In the first portion of this chapter, I will describe the type of community relations initiatives that I typically executed. The next portion of the chapter will describe the performance management systems that I utilized and how the combination of the two systems became a powerful force for student success during my second tenure in Dallas ISD.

Building Strong Community Relations

A leader must have an attitude. If a superintendent wants to make a positive impact on their community, their relentless positive attitude must also come with an unwavering belief in customer service.

Core 4 Customer Service Values

My Core 4 customer service model and mantra is developed around four key values. In rank order, a leader must be:

1. Focused on student achievement—we transform students' lives.

2. Fast in the delivery of products and services—urgency for all.

3. Flexible in the products and services—we strive for the *yes*.

4. Friendly in the approach to all—we make memorable moments.

I asked my team to collect data on the effectiveness of each department and school based upon this framework. The data were quantitative and qualitative and shared with the school and district leaders. The district confronted the facts, even though some were brutal, but never gave up hope. Dallas ISD was transformed from a culture of entitlement to a culture of accountability.

In the mid-1990s, I attended a seminar at the Harvard Business School called Strategic Perspectives in Non-Profit Management. Harvard uses the case study method. The case we studied was the customer service model for Scandinavian Airlines. I took the model and adapted it to public education. I implemented my version in every school system I led for the rest of my career, although it was not until my second tenure in Dallas that it paid significant dividends. Two companies, K12 Insight and Engage2Learn, made the system robust. One helped refine the data, and the other helped to coach for success.

As previously described, the Success Triangle (Figure 1.1) for superintendents places students in the center as its main focus. At the top of the triangle is the board; at the base of the triangle are the teachers, staff, and community. It is imperative that any successful superintendent have a specific strategy for community relations. One veteran superintendent advised me that for him, the staff was his focus. He said the community belonged to the school board. Based on my experience, I learned that his worldview was an over-simplification. While his view has merit, others taught me that it was not that simple. The board should not meddle with the staff, but organic interaction is healthy. Additionally, the superintendent cannot rely on the board alone to handle the community. Board members are typically volunteers and have other full-time obligations. The community is not a monolith.

Governmental Relationships

For a superintendent, one portion of the community is government. The three levels of government are federal, state, and local. At the federal level, the role of the superintendent is typically limited except for rare occasions. The federal government delegates the oversight of education to the states. However, some key federal agencies have a significant impact on the operations of a school district. Trade organizations such as the Council of the Great City Schools and AASA (formerly the American Association of School Administrators) have departments that monitor federal legislation. Child nutrition, technology, and supplemental education services like the Title programs impact school districts that have students living in poverty. Superintendents interact with members of the United States Congress and United States Department of Education on a very limited basis.

State government is much different. Most superintendents have existing relationships with the local legislative delegations in their communities. Public education should be nonpartisan, but it is typically not. Nevertheless, the superintendent should have an effective working relationship with legislators regardless of party affiliation. I used the Nominal Group Technique to assist the school board and staff to develop the legislative priorities for each session. As described in Chapter 3, the Nominal Group Technique is a group brainstorming strategy where everyone writes down their ideas. Then all suggestions are discussed, ranked, and prioritized. This strategy provides an opportunity for everyone's ideas and opinions to be taken into consideration.

For most superintendents, the major involvement with the executive branch of state government is with the state education agency or department. In my twenty-seven years as a superintendent, I had a very close working relationship with every commissioner of education. For me, it was essential to respect the office of the commissioner of education even though the officeholder at any given time might not be someone I respected or agreed with.

At the local level, government is also very important. Depending on the type of school district, the relationship with municipalities varies. Serving a county district is very complex. Multiple jurisdictions must be served—from the county to unincorporated areas, to small towns, to cities, and possibly even a namesake city. Relations with elected officials such as county commissioners and city council members are also complex due to the political nature of those positions. Cultivating a relationship with the head of those elected bodies is very important.

In namesake cities such as Dallas, the relationship with the mayor is critical to the success of both the city and the school district. I maintained a positive working relationship with every mayor of Dallas for my entire thirteen years. At times, the relationship became strained, but it was imperative to maintain a cordial appearance to the public. The leaders of these two important governmental bodies should find ways to agree in public, even if disagreements occur from time to time behind closed doors.

What is often underestimated by superintendents is the relationship with city staff. Dallas executes a "weak mayor" system in which the city manager is the chief executive officer, and the mayor is the chair of the city council. Effective mayors in these types of systems still wield significant influence due to their bully pulpit, but the day-to-day operations of the city are assigned to the city manager by law. Most taxpayers do not understand the independence of governments. They just know that they pay taxes. It is important that the taxpayers see value in their investments regardless of the entity.

In my thirteen years as superintendent of Dallas ISD, I worked with three different city managers who all had distinct leadership styles. I was able to convince all three city managers to have quarterly meetings with our senior staff members. This proved to be one of the most successful community relations activities that I ever utilized. The entities took turns hosting these sessions. Each team would place topics on the agenda that they felt would impact the entire community. These sessions also allowed the staff members to build relationships with key governmental executives in the community. Both entities have significant finance, operations, communications, transportation, and human resource functions. They also must deal with public funds and open meetings and records, not to mention the political drama of the roles. These quarterly meetings allowed both entities to make better, more informed decisions.

In Dallas, there was an additional governmental team, the Ad Hoc Council, that met prior to my arrival and that in my opinion was a stroke of brilliance. It was hosted by the chief executive officer of the Dallas Citizens Council. (The Citizens Council is a super chamber of commerce made up of CEOs of the major companies in Dallas.) The Ad Hoc Council is made up of the Dallas County Judge (executive) who is the only elected official, the city manager of the City of Dallas, the superintendent of the Dallas ISD, the chancellor of Dallas College (community college), the CEO of Parkland Hospital (county), and the CEO of the Dallas Area Rapid Transit System (DART). The group meets once per month for breakfast, with no agenda and no designees. This group built long-standing relationships with other heads of government, did informal planning, and managed community crises, such as the pandemic and extreme weather such as floods, tornadoes, winter storms, and the like. I would strongly recommend to any city superintendent of the largest district in any county to establish such a group if one does not already exist. The collaboration and planning done in these informal meetings is extremely powerful, especially for public servants of goodwill. Keep in mind that not all public servants are of goodwill, but don't let that detail overshadow your willingness to put together your own Ad Hoc Council.

> ## PRO TIP
>
> I would strongly recommend establishing an Ad Hoc Council in your district. The collaboration and planning done in these informal meetings is extremely powerful, especially for public servants of goodwill.

The Kitchen Cabinet

U.S. President Andrew Jackson introduced a concept that I decided to replicate. Instead of just relying on his governmental cabinet to advise him, he met with his most trusted friends and political supporters in an informal way in the White House kitchen. Thus, they became his Kitchen Cabinet. During both of my terms in Dallas ISD, I appointed a Kitchen Cabinet. These were a set of diverse civic leaders who I trusted and respected. I would run ideas by them when big decisions were being contemplated. They advised me of issues they were hearing in the community. They helped raise money for key munic-ipal elections, especially school board and bond elections in which the use of public dollars was prohibited. All members of the Kitchen Cabinet had been or were currently leaders of large, complex orga-nizations. They also helped me with some innovative ideas such as the HiPo Group, described in Chapter 3.

Hinojosa-ism

Complex issues do not have linear solutions.

Grappling with issues such as achievement, funding, and politics at the same time usually requires less than simple solutions and require people to work together to find creative solutions.

Community-Based Organizations and Nonprofits

Community-based organizations and nonprofits are another key aspect of community relationships. Chambers of Commerce are one example and were critical during my entire career in every community I served. Chambers have a vested interest in good schools, because good schools create good communities, which help drive successful businesses. Regional or umbrella chambers are hugely important. An umbrella chamber speaks for the entire region, not just the namesake city. They recruit economic development for all parts of the metroplex, not just within the boundaries of the city. They bring business to local communities, which helps expand the tax base. Even if property values are equalized in a state for maintenance and operations, they are very helpful in debt service. Regardless, they are of great benefit to school districts and superintendents should embrace their support. Ethnic chambers and smaller community chambers also have a valuable role in the support of a school district. Equity in every sense of the word is very important if the superintendent desires a vibrant community.

Similarly, many service-based organizations want to have a voice. The Rotary Club is one example of a service organization that at one time had significant influence in communities across the country but whose voice may be waning. A politically savvy superintendent will make sure to find which organizations carry influence in each community. Be judicious in the allocation of time and effort in the community. The community is at the base of the success triangle, not at the top. Delegating part of this responsibility to key senior staff is a win-win strategy—you can free up some of your very limited time while giving senior staff additional leadership opportunities.

Other civic organizations and nonprofits, such as United Way, also work hand in hand with school districts to bring wrap-around services to the students directly and indirectly. Most collective impact organizations are also useful. They are typically a guiding coalition of like-minded individuals and organizations who believe in public education. Their motives and structures should be evaluated in a case-by-case manner.

Local boards and commissions developed on an ad hoc basis can also be invaluable. During my first tenure in Dallas, I established the Dallas Achieves Commission. This very diverse group of organizations and individuals, including business, unions, and marginalized ethnic and racial groups, devised a report like that of a Base Closing Commission used by the federal government. The understanding was that the recommendations would be taken as a whole, and that cherry picking would not be appropriate. This is probably the only way to get a diverse group of individual constituents to come to consensus.

In every community I served, I also appointed a Business and Community Advisory Committee that I met with quarterly. The members were typically people who had a vested interest in public education that did not belong to any other group. At the meetings I would typically cover three main topics and then take their comments, questions, and concerns. In some communities I formed a diverse Ministerial Alliance and followed the same format.

Grass Roots and Grass Tops

Local communities are unique. This is especially true at the grass roots and the grass tops levels. *Grass roots* are people who have influence deep in the community. Many of these leaders do not have a formal title or position, but they wield significant influence due to the vast number of relationships they have among community members and the true respect they hold, such as a local barber, Sunday school teacher, or small diner owner. In an organic entry plan, a new superintendent may not discover who these people are, but in due time they surface. *Grass tops* people, in my definition, are community members who have a title. They may be the head of the local units of National Association for the Advancement of Colored People (NAACP) or the League of United Latin American Citizens (LULAC), but they do not garner much influence because of their militancy. These people cannot be ignored, whether or not they have the ability to influence the community.

The Importance of Parents

Parents are a key part of the community strategy. The onus of ensuring parental engagement lies with campus principals, but that doesn't mean that the superintendent shouldn't use their influence to encourage parent engagement. I have always been careful about how I characterize the role of parents. My parents did not visit schools when their children were students, yet their ten children and twenty-two grandchildren all received a great education. Parents might not seem involved when you don't see them on campus, but they are involved behind the scenes. Still, I know the value that families bring when they show up, and I wanted parental involvement in schools. With that goal in mind, I set up many systems that facilitated their participation. What I did not want was for any educator to say that they were not responsible for a student's education because the parents were not involved. My view is that educators are ultimately responsible for student learning—parents are our partners on that adventure—but it is our responsibility in the end.

Transparency Through Performance Management

Few superintendents would put performance management in the same chapter with community relations. I can see that point of view, but I have been accused of being a contrarian superintendent. It's a label I agree with and carry with pride. Being accountable to the community is an important part of being a superintendent, and being honest with your performance evaluation is one way to be fully transparent and accountable.

Superintendent Performance Evaluation

During my first twelve years as a superintendent, my performance evaluation was 100 percent confidential. The board president and the board would meet without me to discuss my performance. Afterwards, the chair would debrief me for about fifteen minutes. My evaluations were generally good. The board would then vote to extend my contract for another year. I would love to say that I was happy with the process, but I really wasn't. I received no substantive feedback, and the district just moved forward to another year.

That all changed during my first term as superintendent in Dallas. The board president was a man named Jack Lowe, who had been the chief executive officer for TD Industries for decades. TD Industries is the largest and most successful heating, ventilation, and air conditioning (HVAC) company in North Texas. They operated the HVAC systems for most office buildings in downtown Dallas. At the same time, he was the board president for several major corporations. I shared with him how frustrated I was with my evaluation process, results, and lack of clarity.

Hinojosa-ism

If you are working on something important, involve the stakeholders, and follow a process that will take you to the eventual product.

Involving stakeholders is key, and you must have processes to balance power relationships to ensure that the final product is substantive with significant ownership.

President Lowe, who insisted on being called Jack, appointed a subcommittee of the board to develop a new instrument. He appointed himself as chair and introduced the form and process he had used on several corporate boards. My staff and I participated in every session as the design was laid out. My new evaluation system went from 100 percent subjective to 96 percent objective. For most of the last fifteen years as a superintendent, I knew what I was going to be held accountable for and where the system was headed.

The structure varied slightly in Dallas ISD and Cobb County School District (where I spent my last sixteen years as superintendent before retiring), but overall, the instrument stayed the same. Sixty percent of my evaluation was based on student outcomes. The board would identify SMART student outcomes (specific, measurable, achievable, relevant, and time-bound), set targets, fund the initiatives, and hold me accountable for the results. The targets were based on a five-year historical performance. The board and the staff (me) would have to agree on what attainable performance would be. The targets included a performance measure that included the opportunity to earn partial credit. I could be deemed "Somewhat Successful" if performance increased to a certain level. Below that level, zero points were awarded, and I was determined to have been "Unsuccessful" on that goal. If I met the target, I was deemed to be "Fully Successful" and was awarded the entire point value. If the target was exceeded by a significant level, I was awarded bonus points and deemed to be "Clearly Superior." The system and the goals brought coherence and drive to a large, complex system.

Holding the Superintendent Accountable

Implement yearly evaluations based on mutually agreed-upon, reasonable, and measurable goals. For example, the evaluation can include the following elements:

60% Student outcomes

20% Financial stewardship

20% Stakeholder satisfaction

(Continued)

(Continued)

4% Students (customers)

4% Parents (customers)

4% Staff

4% Taxpayers (owners)

4% School board

The second section of my evaluation was financial stewardship, and a similar process was developed to arrive at reasonable targets. The Dallas ISD had an unflattering history regarding financial stewardship that became impeccable by the time I retired. This section was publicly reported and was 20 percent of my evaluation.

The final 20 percent of my evaluation was stakeholder satisfaction; it comprised success in addressing the needs of five key groups of stakeholders: the students (customers), parents (customers), the staff, the taxpayers (owners), and the school board, each representing 4 percent. The section from the school board was the only confidential portion of my evaluation. The district had fully transformed from a culture of entitlement to a culture of accountability. This was the beginning of the establishment of true performance reporting management.

School Performance Management and Accountability

In the last decade, the sweeping strategy to adopt the A–F system of rating schools and districts became intense. Texas had always rated schools in categories, but now a proposal included the F "scarlet letter" to be assigned to the worst schools in the state. As the legislation was being proposed by the Commissioner of Education, I testified vehemently against the legislation early and often. At the eleventh hour, a compromise was introduced that local districts could develop alternatives that became known as a Local Accountability System (LAS). The system would have to be approved by the commissioner. Approximately fifteen districts started working together on the system. Eventually, only Dallas ISD and Snyder ISD, a small district in west Texas, adopted their own LAS. Snyder ISD was under some kind of state monitoring by the Texas Education Agency due to their lack of achievement. Snyder dropped their system after a short period of implementation.

As of this writing, the LAS still exists in Dallas. The Dallas ISD and community not only believed in and supported accountability, but we also felt that it should be robust, fair, and more rigorous than the state. I am an optimistic person and argue that you cannot shame people into doing the right thing. You must motivate them on the importance of being accountable and owning it. At the elementary level, the entire system was based upon the state exam. At the secondary level it included college, career, and military readiness. The multiple measures also included quantifiable data, such as graduation rates.

PRO TIP

You cannot shame people into doing the right thing. You must motivate them on the importance of being accountable and owning it.

The state required the LAS to have 50 percent of its value to be the state accountability system. We complied. Thirty percent of the system was based on value-added performance. Since the 1990s, Dallas ISD has used the School Effectiveness Index (SEI), which compared schools and teachers (CEI) with similar circumstances and demographics. It developed an expected score based upon these regression elements. This leveled the playing field; magnet schools had to exceed their expected performance, and high-poverty schools got credit for significant progress (growth) even if they did not meet the absolute performance target. This forced educators to never just focus on the "bubble" students. The bubble concept was malpractice: "Get these students to pass and move to the next category. Forget the others they are not passing anyway." The SEI created a fair but complex system that rewarded educators for focusing on each individual student. This value-added system became 30 percent of the campus rating.

Hinojosa-ism

In God we trust. All others must bring data.

When making important decisions, both quantitative and qualitative data must be considered.

The remaining 20 percent of the accountability system is based upon voice and the student experience. Ten percent of the system is based on parent and staff surveys of how they rate the culture of the school and district. Peter Drucker, a management consultant and editor, once quipped "culture eats strategy for breakfast." I wholeheartedly agree. The final 10 percent is the student experience. This includes not only surveys but also participation in extracurricular activities.

This final 10 percent serves to provide checks and balances so that principals and schools consider the "whole child" and not just a score or number. In my experience as a superintendent, I have had to release leaders who lost their religion chasing a number. This rating system was more rigorous than the state. We had fewer schools rated at the top levels of performance than if we had only used the state criteria.

Another profound element of LAS emanated from my disdain of the A–F system, especially the "scarlet letter" (F). Instead of rating a school an A, the district rating is Accomplished. Instead of a B, the district rating is Breakthrough. Instead of a C, Dallas ISD's rating is Competing. Instead of D, the district rating is Developing. Instead of a F, the district rating is Focused. Focused campuses received substantial additional resources in the form of funds and support. They have very little autonomy under the district's theory of action called Managed Instruction With Earned Empowerment. This is further evidence that community relations impacts performance management. The state had a rule that you could not "local" your way out of a D or an F. We still called them Developed and Focused, but officially they were D and F.

Public School Choice in Dallas ISD is another strategic initiative in which the district partners with the community to create start-up transformation schools that by design integrate the schools to provide transparency and accountability. The following entities partnered

with the Dallas ISD Office of Transformation and Innovation to create
a start-up public school:

1. Toyota Corporation
2. Southern Methodist University
3. Dallas College
4. Paul Quinn College (a historically Black university)
5. University of Texas Southwestern Medical Center
6. Texas A&M Commerce
7. North Dallas Chamber
8. Downtown Dallas Incorporated

Many individuals in the community also participated in public school
choice. This is another example of performance management via
community involvement.

The Big Ideas

Being a successful superintendent means building strong community
relations and promoting transparency in performance reporting. Here
are the big ideas I shared in Chapter 4:

▶ **The community is multifaceted.**
   The community is complex and made up of many different
   sectors—government, civic, and family. As the superintendent
   you likely do not have time to attend to all aspects, so delegate
   to trusted key staff members.

▶ **It's important to learn your local structure.**
   It is vital that you understand how your community
   works—from the city and government agencies to the civic
   and non-profit organizations. Who are the decision makers?
   Where does money come from? Where or who do people go to
   when there are problems? Once you understand how it works,
   you can figure out how you fit into the puzzle to best serve the
   needs of the students and families in your district.

▶ **Accountability and transparency through
   performance management are essential.**
   Although it might feel uncomfortable to let all stakeholders
   weigh in on your performance publicly, in doing so you build
   trust, accountability, and credibility and everyone wins in
   the end.

▶ **Fair and transparent school accountability is attainable.**
When you take into consideration multiple aspects of performance—not just academics—you can better serve the needs of students. And educators will feel more supported because they aren't being judged purely by test scores.

CHAPTER #4

Reflect and Act

Now it's time to reflect on what you've read and decide how you can best apply the insights gained from the chapter in practical ways within your district. Use this modified "five 'A's" protocol (Agree, Argue, Apply, Actions, and Accountable) to journal your ideas.

What do you **agree** with in the chapter?	What do you want to **argue** about within the chapter?
How can you **apply** the information from this chapter to your own district?	What **actions** can you take after reading this chapter? And how will you hold yourself **accountable**?

Adapted from Judith Gray, "Four 'A's Text Protocol," National School Reform Faculty (2005), www.nsrfharmony.org.

CHAPTER 5

Work Toward Academic Excellence

Academic excellence is the main thing, and keeping the main thing the main thing is paramount. Superintendents must understand how teaching and learning works. By design, the previous chapters have helped establish the systems that should be in place for academic achievement to flourish. In the same way that very few head football coaches can simultaneously be the head coach and offensive coordinator, very few superintendents can successfully navigate being both the chief executive officer and the chief academic officer. However, even a non-educator who serves as superintendent of schools must know how teaching and learning works.

Implementing Your Theory of Action

The theory of action of the school district is its value proposition. Every district has one, but very few are articulated clearly. A school district is either a school system or system of schools. A *school system* believes in managed instruction. A *system of schools* believes in performance empowerment. There are very few districts that are at these extremes. Most districts are somewhere in between. The Dallas ISD had a very clearly defined theory of action known as Managed Instruction With Earned Empowerment. It started with a board policy adopted originally in 2007 but not fully executed until my second tenure as superintendent in about 2017.

The premise behind a system of schools is that the individuals closest to the students should have the authority to make decisions regarding teaching and learning, as well as many other systems that directly affect those within each school. Thus, performance empowerment theory believes that educators and leaders should be granted autonomy as a motivator. The principal and staff select the curriculum, instructional materials, professional development, and more. They believe that given these autonomies, achievement will flourish over time. This is also known as the decentralized model. There are very few decentralized districts; most of them are large and urban. Some examples are New York, Chicago, Los Angeles, Houston, Denver, Clark County (Nevada), and New Orleans. The biggest promise is that autonomy encourages freedom and innovation. The concern is the Swiss cheese curriculum—the written, taught, and assessed curriculum has many holes. Highly mobile students fall further behind when they move to different schools with different curricular offerings and processes. As an example, different schools in the same district may have different math programs. Many concepts in math are sequential. A prerequisite skill may have already been taught when the highly mobile student moves to a new building.

The premise behind a school system of managed instruction is that every system is tightly managed to ensure compliance, alignment, and coherence. The written, taught, and assessed curriculum are in alignment and centralized. The central office staff has the content expertise to access deeper knowledge due to the specialized nature of instructional specialists and coaches. The greatest promise is that coherence will lead to alignment and achievement. The concern is that these processes are bureaucratic and stifle innovation and academic freedom. Most rural, town, and suburban districts closely follow a managed instruction theory of action. As stated earlier, there are very few districts at the extremes.

Most school districts are somewhere in the middle. The problem is that school districts rarely define their theory of action. This lack of clarity leads to significant confusion especially when there are numerous leadership transitions. Every new leader enters with their own worldview and set of experiences. In my professional opinion, the school board should determine the *what*, with guidance from the administrative staff. In this case, the *what* is the theory of action. Then it is the job of the administration to execute the *how*. This is what administration is all about. The administration is paid to execute on the vision, mission, and goals. Elected officials determine the overall direction via governance and oversight. Leadership and management are responsible for execution and implementation.

Under my leadership and direction, the Dallas ISD developed a theory of action playbook that is thorough and transparent. The Local Accountability System, explained in Chapter 4, is the cornerstone for Managed Instruction With Earned Empowerment. All schools get significant systems of support and resources that are clearly delineated by every division. Competing, Developing, and Focus schools get more resources and systems of support and virtually no autonomies. Breakthrough schools get some autonomies, with Accomplished schools getting the most.

By design, the schools that perform well on specific measures are granted limited autonomies because the results prove that they are effective. The schools that do not perform at that level get a lot of love. The love is identified as direction and resources with very little variation. Dallas ISD Board Policy AE (LOCAL) clearly defines the mission, vision, core values, student outcome goals, constraints and progress measures, strategic covenants, and the theory of action.

By being codified in such a significant fashion, it sets the direction for how the system will be governed, managed, and led.

Academic Expectations

George W. Bush famously warned about the danger of "the soft bigotry of low expectations." In Spanish, we refer to this as the *pobresito* syndrome. The phrase is loosely translated as "you poor child." High expectations are nonnegotiable. However, high expectations without support is cruelty; support without expectations is chaos. To illustrate this point, sometimes when I speak to large groups of people, I tell them that I have high expectations that everyone in the room can do fifty pushups. This is high expectations without support. I know that most of them cannot get to ten. However, given time, weight training, and proper nutrition, at some time in the future everyone will be able to get there unless they have a severe physical disability. The same is true for academic achievement. When we put structures in place that facilitate learning and communicate high expectations, students will succeed.

> ## PRO TIP
>
> Have high expectations for everyone—students and staff. Provide necessary supports. Put structures in place to facilitate learning and communicate high expectations clearly and often so that everyone knows what you think they can accomplish.

I visited Yselta ISD to see in action how they were accomplishing such incredible academic success. Much of it was due to tremendously high expectations and significant teacher and student support to execute that vision. As a result of that experience, I developed the Great Expectations Framework for Dallas ISD, and we used that framework to shift mindsets around expectations across the district. The framework included the following big ideas:

- Expect the best from staff and students.

- All communities are special (no such thing as "those" kids or "those" neighborhoods).

- Have an abundance mentality by believing in the art of the possible.

Those same expectations exist for the board, the staff, and the community. I expressed that expectation for our school facilities as well. Even if the building was old, it must be clean and smell fresh. That is within our sphere of control. Suburban parents have high expectations for facilities, so why shouldn't everyone? It is difficult to learn if the physical environment is dirty, unpleasant, too hot, or too cold.

Academic Systems

I learned a very valuable lesson during my time as superintendent in a smaller Texas school district. Being on the executive committee of the Texas Association of School Administrators, I was exposed to many educational products and services. I employed a service provider who executed a curriculum management audit, which nearly cost me my job. The model that this organization used was a deficit audit. It was accurate but harsh in the deficits it found.

The audit studied every system in the district, including maintenance, that could impact student learning. It provided no commendations; instead, it provided dozens of recommendations about how to improve academic achievement. This very proud school district, which had outstanding athletic and music programs, was not in the mood to hear how sorry they were in academics, such as having no formal written curriculum. The audit was not inaccurate, but it divided the community—pitting people who had lived in the county for decades against residents newer to the area.

The irony is that the district implemented almost all the recommendations with significant success. My tenure was even able to survive a "coup" by some of the board members to get rid of me because I dared to implement some significant changes. However, many in the community supported the changes and rallied around them. The experience had such an impact on me that I decided to do an interactive qualitative analysis of other superintendents who served during these deficit audits as the focus of my doctoral dissertation work. I interviewed ten superintendents who had more than three years of experience in their district at the time of the audit and ten who were relatively new to their district, defined as less than fifteen months experience in their district. The findings were not a surprise. Very few of the superintendents who had significant tenure were able to survive the deficit nature of the audits, even if the recommendations benefitted the system. Superintendents are accountable for everything. Most of the negative reports happened under their watch. Most of the superintendents in districts in which the audit was done early in their tenure survived and some thrived. But the interviews revealed that the upheaval created a significant impact on the culture, climate, and conflict in the system. When I became the superintendent of the Dallas ISD, I asked for an audit but from a different firm that did not utilize deficit audits. This firm provided commendations and recommendations that were not harsh in their language and thus more readily accepted.

Having objective information from a trusted external partner can be very useful in addressing issues in the district as a new superintendent. It is also critically important to not insult the professionals who developed and are implementing the current initiatives, which may need to be revised or completely redone. Being honest is important, being harsh is not necessary. Many superintendents are incredulous about what they inherit. Rather than whine about it, it is important to solve problems.

Hinojosa-ism

Be honest but not harsh.

Too many people are afraid to be direct about an issue. Information that is conveyed directly is seldom misunderstood. Hurting people's feeling makes people reticent to accept feedback.

Professional Learning

I am proud to have been an athletic coach. The true coaching model can have a significant impact on academic achievement. I have a contrarian's view of mentoring and coaching. If I am assigned a coach who I do not respect, I will not engage meaningfully, and I don't believe that I'm the only person who feels this way. For a coaching relationship to work, it must be built on mutual respect and working toward desired goals or outcomes. I posit that human nature controls the psyche of most individuals. You will seldom tell your boss that you do not know how to do something. But you will readily ask a trusted colleague, mentor, or coach when you need assistance.

Instructional coaching has tremendous promise if done well. It demonstrates a true commitment to training to retain high-quality educators. Traditional professional development has mixed results at best. The one-time stand and deliver professional development workshops have almost no chance of success. The coaching model in which strategies are attempted in small doses with meaningful feedback given on a consistent basis will typically have a greater impact. Not all great teachers make great instructional coaches. Many of them don't know why they are great. The same is true in sports. Very few superstar players have become successful coaches.

Instructional coaches need training and support as well. Content expertise is important but not sufficient. There is an art and science to coaching, just like teaching. The coaching industry has become so sophisticated that there are now tools available that document all the activities in the coaching cycle. The coaching model applies to teachers, coaches, principals, and all leaders.

The principal must be an instructional leader on the campus. I consistently tell principals, "I am not the superintendent, it is the superintendency; you are not the principal, it is the principalship." The principal is the captain of the ship. During my first tenure in Dallas, my outstanding chief academic officer convinced me that the only way to build the academic prowess of the principalship was via academic institutes. See Chapter 4 for information about the community-focused version of Dallas Achieves, which the Boston Consulting Group helped organize.

During my first tenure, the districtwide turnaround strategy was called Dallas Achieves. The staff was led by Dr. Denise Collier, the chief academic officer, who developed, organized, and executed over twenty-five Dallas Achieves institutes. We partnered with the Institute for Learning, which produced significant rigor, accountable talk, and a common language that became the foundation of the institutes.

Every campus was required to have the principal, at least one assistant principal, and the Campus Instructional Leadership Team (CILT) be part of the ship. The CILT composition was different at the various levels of schools, such as elementary and secondary schools. At the elementary schools the CILT included grade-level leaders and content instructional coaches. At the secondary level it included department chairs and instructional coaches.

As the superintendent, I attended each of these sessions. I did the kick-off and participated in as many of the sessions as possible.

I wanted to send a message that this was important to me and thus it should be important to all these instructional leaders. I get a lot of credit for improving academic achievement during my second tenure, deservedly or not. But much of the academic blocking and tackling occurred during my first tenure. Many of the teachers in the Dallas Achieves institutes during my first tenure became principals during my second tenure. Many principals during my first became district leaders during my second. Many in both tenures have become superintendents. Training staff and developing potential really pays off over time.

Mirrors or Windows

For an independent study of how Dallas ISD and other school districts had success in overcoming the effects of poverty and improving student achievement, see the Council of the Great City Schools publication, *Mirrors or Windows* (June 2021). https://www.cgcs.org/Page/1288

Urgency and Turnaround Strategies

Turnaround initiatives and strategies for individual schools in academic triage in an urban context are extremely vital. During my first tenure at the Dallas ISD, I was summoned to Washington, DC, along with about fifteen other urban superintendents to meet with the Secretary of Education. In my naïveté, I thought they wanted to hear about our turnaround strategy that seemed to be working. Instead, they wanted to convince us to adopt a model that the U.S. Department of Education had developed using School Improvement Grants. Turnaround models work when the customized needs of individual communities are met.

Miami Dade County School District, under the direction of Superintendent Alberto Carvalho, had a turnaround process that produced significant results. Portions of the process have been replicated with success in other school districts where protégés of Superintendent Carvalho have become superintendents. A powerful protocol in the strategy is known as Datacom. The protocol includes the principal of the lowest-performing school having a meeting with the superintendent. Other principals are in the bullpen (the room) watching the process until it is their turn. The superintendent's senior team attends the meeting as well but does not participate until directed. The principal presents achievement data along with a plan to solve the problem. The superintendent asks what barriers need to be overcome for the plan to succeed. The superintendent then directs the senior staff to remove those barriers to success. The process is repeated on a regular basis. The results of this initiative have been outstanding. Miami is one of the highest-performing districts in the country, with very few low-performing schools. The model has been replicated in many urban districts with significant success.

During my first tenure in Dallas, I put all the lowest-performing schools in one network or learning community. In very large districts the principals cannot report to the superintendent. They report to principal supervisors in either feeder patterns, grade alignments, or geographic organizers. During my first tenure in Dallas, I organized the schools in geographical learning communities, such as the West Learning Community. The one exception was the Superintendent's Learning Community. It was a symbolic gesture that I was responsible for the lowest-performing schools. I hired a former principal who had significant experience in turning around failing schools. He hired a team of talented leaders who would bring focus to the struggling schools. I met with him and his team every Friday afternoon. Since he reported to me, he had access to all the district's resources to help these struggling schools.

Initially, schools did not want to be in the Superintendent's Learning Community because of the stigma of being a struggling school. Multiple data sets including culture and climate were used as the criteria to qualify. But, as principals realized the types of additional resources that were available, "membership" in the learning community was not perceived quite as negatively as it had been initially. Membership in the learning community was fluid. If achievement accelerated to a significant level, the school moved into the geographical learning community the following year. Jack Welch, CEO of General Electric, was notorious for terminating the bottom 10 percent of employees. There is always a bottom 10 percent. The same was true in Dallas ISD schools. The difference is that we did not fire you—we fired you up!

During my second tenure the turnaround strategy was completely different and even more effective. The lowest-performing schools in Texas have always been publicly identified. Such labels include Academically Unacceptable, Improvement Required, and now the scarlet letter F. Between my first and second tenures at Dallas ISD the state adopted a new test and accountability system. When I came back to Dallas ISD in 2015, the district had forty-six failing schools. In my second entry plan it became strongly evident that school turn-around would be of high priority almost immediately. Multiple strategies were required, and they worked. By the time the pandemic hit, there were only four F schools in Dallas ISD.

My team and I studied the data and determined that two district turnaround solutions would be implemented. There was a large group of schools that would require structure and guidance similar to the original Superintendent's Learning Community. I hired the same administrator and he "put the band back together." About thirty schools were put into this group, which we called Improved School Network (ISN). In two years, he and his team were able to get almost all those schools to a level of C or D. He worked his way out of a job and was given another assignment in the district.

The second turnaround strategy was the Accelerating Campus Excellence (ACE) restructuring model developed by the Charlotte-Mecklenburg school district in North Carolina. The ACE model included no incrementalism. It was a very comprehensive deep overhaul of a school from top to bottom—a very controversial solution to a very persistent problem. Every employee on the identified campuses was required to reapply for their jobs. None of the incumbent principals were selected to remain. Outstanding, experienced principals were selected and given a significant financial stipend to take on these schools. Almost without exception, 95 percent of the employees selected were not incumbents.

There are some significant differences between the ACE model and any other ones previously attempted. Most models included having outstanding principals sent to a school. The biggest difference was the "B" teacher. The "B" teachers would tell the new principal, "I will be here when you are gone." As a superintendent I, at times, committed academic malpractice. I would hire new, inexperienced teachers and place them in tough schools and wonder why they left, many times before the end of the year. The great principal could now select every employee, including the school secretary. The principal received an additional $15,000 to go to the ACE school. The teachers received an additional $10,000 each. One thousand dollars won't change behavior but

$10,000 will, especially if it will count toward retirement. But these teachers had to be great teachers.

PRO TIP

Place great administrators and great teachers at sites where they can make the most significant impact.

The incumbent teachers had contracts. Very few teachers were ever terminated for cause. Most left and went to other districts. The ones who did not leave were reassigned to other campuses. No school was forced to take more than three teachers from these failing schools. Many of these teachers had not learned the art and science of teaching, but they flourished in less stressful schools.

The ACE model had an extended school day and school year. Both of which were scaled back due to intense burnout and the hard, long work. The ACE model worked as promised. In one year virtually every school moved to a C or better. One school, which had been underperforming twelve out of thirteen years, went to a B in one year and an A in the second year. Same students, same parents, and same neighborhoods. Success happens when you bring talent to the 'hood!

Hinojosa-ism

If everything is important, nothing is important.

Focusing on a few key strategic initiatives is the only thing that gets results.

Staff and Train Strategically

As the superintendent, you must hire the right people for every position. Two of the most critical are the chief of schools and chief academic officer. The one regret I have is that it took me too long to realize that you need to have one person, such as a deputy superintendent, to oversee these two roles. The chief of schools wants to protect principals' time and the chief academic officer wants access to give them the good stuff. If I could do it over, I would have hired a deputy superintendent sooner.

Every district has different titles, but whoever oversees teaching and learning needs to ensure that the technical structures are in place, such as curriculum, instruction, and assessment. Scope and sequence and pacing guides are critical to having a coherent academic program. Certain subjects have prerequisites that must be addressed at the proper grade levels. High-stakes accountability has created an overabundance of testing. However, some forms of interim assessments are necessary to clearly determine progress in achievement. Both absolute achievement and growth have value and must be balanced in a fair assessment program.

Similarly, professional learning systems must be in place to ensure academic success. Professional learning communities (PLCs) can be effective structures and systems to develop talent, but only if they are properly designed and executed. The focus of any PLC must be academic. Operational matters should be handled via other means, such as written procedures and protocols. The superintendent must ensure that a coherent academic plan is in place and is monitored regularly.

For twenty-seven years, I visited schools on Wednesdays. This disciplined practice sent a message that schools and academic programs were very important to me. Reviewing the school data prior to entering the building gave me an anticipatory set of things to look for on the tour. At staff meetings I could recall issues that we reviewed at individual schools. I truly believe it gave me a competitive advantage over leaders who did not visit schools regularly. It also gave me credibility with principals because I was seeing the academic program from the ground floor. Walking in their shoes always paid significant dividends.

The Big Ideas

Being a successful superintendent means staying focused on academic achievement even when there are many distractions vying for your attention. Here are the big ideas I shared in Chapter 5:

> ▶ **Academic excellence is what it's all about.**
> In the end, academics is the main thing. It's why students are at the center of the Success Triangle. Everything else I've shared in the previous chapters, while extremely important, is the means to this end.

▶ **You aren't in control, but ultimately you are accountable.**
You aren't the one spending time in front of students every day, but the systems and expectations and structures you put in place are what enable everyone else to be successful.

▶ **High expectations with strong support are key.**
The only way high expectations will be met is to provide teachers and students with the resources and training they need to be successful. High expectations without support is cruelty and will only lead to increased teacher turnover in your district and low academic performance.

▶ **Don't be afraid to turn schools around.**
We say insanity is doing the same thing over and over again while expecting different results. If schools are continuing to fail year over year, nothing is going to change unless educators do something radically different. I shared two ways we addressed school turnaround in Dallas ISD. Consider your schools and your student population's needs and use the smartest people in your district to make a change!

CHAPTER #5

Reflect and Act

Now it's time to reflect on what you've read and decide how you can best apply the insights gained from the chapter in practical ways within your district. Use this modified "five 'A's" protocol (Agree, Argue, Apply, Actions, and Accountable) to journal your ideas.

What do you **agree** with in the chapter?	What do you want to **argue** about within the chapter?
How can you **apply** the information from this chapter to your own district?	What **actions** can you take after reading this chapter? And how will you hold yourself **accountable**?

Adapted from Judith Gray, "Four 'A's Text Protocol," National School Reform Faculty (2005), www.nsrfharmony.org.

CHAPTER 6

Create a Culture of Efficiency Through a High-Level View of Operations

While student achievement is the main thing, operations—if not handled well—can become the biggest thorn in your side. Most new superintendents are very insecure regarding all facets of operations because they typically have little experience in the business and technology side of the superintendency. Most superintendents are former principals. Principals know school leadership very well. It is their core competence. They have run schools and understand the intricacies of school operations, from running a master schedule to the complexities of extracurricular activities.

As principals are promoted to the central office, they become members of leadership teams. As they advance in their careers, they get to learn many facets of running a school system that are beyond their departments and divisions. In my experience, most leaders do not have a keen interest in operations for a variety of reasons. Operations are not glamorous and are quite often a nuisance.

Finance

Very few jobs in public education are highly technical. I believe that a great leader who is humble, hungry, and smart can do almost any job. Having a core set of knowledge and skills to transfer that knowledge along with a positive attitude can go a long way to ensure success. The one position that *is* highly technical is the chief financial officer (CFO). In smaller districts this role is typically called the business manager.

Most educators scoff when people say that school districts should be run like a business. But it is a business—a big business. School districts typically have one of the largest budgets in any community and are one of the largest employers. School districts deal with public tax dollars, which requires government accounting. A private sector CFO who has not dealt with government accounting must make some major workflow and policy adaptations to be an effective school district finance officer. Every school district must employ an external auditor to audit the finances of the district on an annual basis. In addition, most large districts also have an internal auditor and a department that typically reports to the school board. Most districts produce a document called the Annual Comprehensive Financial Report (ACFR), which is typically prepared by the finance department with some oversight from the external auditors; it is then approved by the school board.

There are too many issues to understand regarding finance, but I will highlight a few of the big ones that every superintendent must have a surface-level working knowledge of early in their tenure in order to be successful.

Revenue and Expenses

Typically, there are three major sources of revenue depending on the property wealth of the district and economic status of the students. These sources are federal, state, and local. Most federal funds are based on the free and reduced-price lunch (FRPL) status of the students. These are typically in the form of grants that are reimbursable after the expenditure to supplement the educational experience of the students but not supplant or replace the state and local dollars allocated to fund their education. Depending on the property wealth of the local community, the amount of state and local funds is equalized to a certain degree, which varies from state to state. The more revenue the district receives from local property taxes, the less state aid they will receive and vice versa. The budget must be adopted by fund and function. Expenditures are then coded accordingly. The codes identify the amount and percentage of the budget spent on every function, such as instruction, administration, transportation, school leadership, maintenance, and so on. These data are recorded by the state and publicly reported so that comparisons among districts can be made.

Taxes

Most states have three sources of tax revenue: sales taxes, property taxes, and income taxes. Texas and several other states do not collect state income tax from residents; therefore, the other taxes are higher. Sales taxes are regressive, thus putting a high proportional burden on people of less wealth. Most states have two tax rates—Maintenance and Operations—which fund salaries and other operational expenses. The other is Interest and Sinking, which can only be used for capital projects and to repay the debt. In a few states, such as Georgia, some districts have no debt because they can have a referendum and use sales taxes to pay for capital projects with cash. Some state governments assist districts with capital projects. Some county, city, and municipal districts are dependent on local government funds and thus have no taxing authority.

Budgeting

In the majority of districts, budgeting is a cyclical process that has various milestones. Most districts have a fiscal year that runs from July 1 to June 30. Others have a fiscal year that runs from September 1 to August 31. The budget for the subsequent year must be adopted prior to the end of the current fiscal year. A current budget report is given to the school board on a monthly basis to monitor expenses and revenue. Budget assumptions include student enrollment, staffing, estimated revenue, and planned expenditures.

A budget calendar is developed with most districts starting budget planning in October for the next school year, but the intensity of the budget planning ramps up in the late winter and early spring. The budget should be the financial plan for the educational program. I have heard some educators claim that they have a zero-based budget of which I am highly skeptical because approximately 85 percent of the expenditures are payroll related. Another 5 percent is assigned to utilities. Therefore, approximately 90 percent of the expenditures are fixed costs that would probably require the termination of either an employment or service contract. There are significant legal risks with termination of contracts prior to the end of the term.

There is a process called strategic abandonment in which certain programs can be sunset through natural attrition. In most districts there is at least a 10 percent turnover rate of employees annually. If only mission-critical positions are filled when they become vacant, then those funds can be redirected for the subsequent fiscal year. That is precisely what we did when the Dallas ISD, under my direction, laid off a thousand employees in October 2008 due to a budget shortfall. We were then able to rehire 600 of those individuals by the next summer. A strategic hiring freeze can redirect funds to other priorities as well.

PRO TIP

For effective budget management, make it a practice to regularly evaluate programs so that you can use the process of strategic abandonment to discontinue programs that are no longer contributing to the district's theory of action.

Position control is a vital system to monitor the status of the budget. The human resources department creates a position only after the finance department has allocated the funds. Very few districts rigorously monitor the status of positions on a regular basis. One person in finance typically manages the position control function, but it should be reviewed by senior staff at least once per month. The school board should also receive monthly reports as an effective oversight of their fiducial function.

The payroll function is extremely vital to any school system since salaries and benefits are the lion share of expenditures. In one school system that I worked in, ghost employees were paid because proper checks and balances were not in place between the finance and human resources departments. There have been numerous controversies nationwide when districts switch from one payroll technology system to another without properly testing the functionality of the new system.

If the general ledger is not reconciled on a very regular basis, then problems are inevitable. This lack of oversight is also a symptom that there are major system flaws in the financial accounting of the district. Some people do not reconcile their personal bank accounts and get away with it. But this is very dangerous when dealing with government funds, and the risks are significant.

There are many types of different funds in government accounting. The general fund is the largest, but there are other categorical funds that have unique purposes and stakeholders. Most systems have bond funds that can only be used for capital expenses. Rules and nuances need to be adhered to, such as not borrowing and amortizing beyond the shelf life of items of purchase, such as technology, buses, and the like. Through experience, superintendents learn what to ask if they pay attention. Novice superintendents are hesitant to show their ignorance in public, and that is understandable. Work with your finance team behind closed doors early and often to get all your questions answered.

Another major budgeting function is procurement. Teachers and principals want products and services when they need them. But as a governmental entity, there are so many requirements that purchasing becomes complex. Running a school system that had a culture of entitlement and numerous major scandals in Dallas created significant issues to overcome. It was not until my final year as superintendent that the system was transformed. It is embarrassing that it took thirteen years to finally resolve such an important business function, but all it took was a major consulting firm funded with philanthropic dollars, which allowed the district to finally develop an efficient plan.

I was fortunate to go from knowing almost nothing about school finance to hanging out at the Capitol and listening to hearings in committee rooms of the Texas Legislature to better understand key terminology and concepts. I testified in a school finance lawsuit against the State of Texas. I know some leaders feel paralyzed just thinking about some of the complexities, but if you give it time and patience, the concepts are not as mysterious or intimidating as you might think.

Facilities Construction and Maintenance

School buildings have a huge impact on students' ability to learn. Some superintendents do not pay enough attention to school facilities, which is understandable considering all the other competing priorities. The churn of superintendents further exacerbates this problem. Facilities are a long-term issue due to the life span of bricks and mortar. If buildings last fifty to seventy-five years and superintendents last fifty to seventy-five months, then the disconnect is obvious. The chief operating officer is typically responsible for school facilities. But external funding is required to build, maintain, and operate facilities, so the superintendent must also be involved beyond a superficial role.

Execution of the existing bond program is the best insurance that the taxpayers will give an opportunity for future programs. An external bond oversight advisory committee made up of diverse stakeholders should be in place to ensure that the program is executed as promised. Internal oversight of architects, contractors, and engineers is critical. Construction staff members will try to convince leadership that program managers are an unnecessary expense. While that sentiment may be accurate on a small program, program managers are critical on large and complex programs.

Superintendents come and go. Board members come and go. COOs come and go. This explains why few school districts have a long-term facilities master plan. A new superintendent during the first hundred days should ask to review the master plan. If one does not exist, then the new superintendent should immediately launch its development. It was not until my return to Dallas, in my twentieth year as a superintendent, that I did so, with much regret. Technology is part of everything in a school system. Before the facilities master plan is developed, a long-range technology plan must also be in place.

Hinojosa-ism

Hope is not a strategy.

Vision, planning, and execution will ensure that systems work as designed.

Management information systems (MIS) is critical to the life-blood of any major organization, especially a school district. From academic performance to the payroll system, information must be readily available, pristine, and easy to use. There are many providers of these products and services. There are very few that operate exclusively in the public education space. Many of the providers adapt the systems used in business and industry to education; many products and services are oversold to educators and underutilized. These legacy systems are critically important but have very few champions. Data management and storage issues are critical. As solutions evolve, it is imperative that IT keeps senior management informed of the latest trends. The chief technology/information officer should always be on the senior staff.

Another MIS consideration is infrastructure and devices. This is such an investment that due diligence must be done from the beginning. The types of infrastructure that exist need to be inventoried. Emerging technologies such as cloud computing must be explored. Attention to cybersecurity must be part of any planning effort. Hardware, software, and devices must be part of any plan if proper execution is to become a reality.

PRO TIP

The advent of artificial intelligence (AI) must be embraced. Savvy superintendents should aggressively study the impact AI can have on instruction and operations.

Instructional Technology

Instructional technology is a completely different lane with similar importance. There are many great products and services available in public education that are typically oversold and underutilized. Having a coherent academic plan and strategy is imperative for there to be efficiency. Stakeholders must be involved in solutions to these issues.

So how does all of this come together for a superintendent who has competing priorities and very little time to get results? Your staff is very busy and has other responsibilities. You can hire a construction or technology firm, but they may have a vested interest in the outcome of the plan, and this could be a slippery slope wrought with ethical dilemmas. There are many consulting firms that can deliver a long-range technology plan, but your specification for the scope and process are critical. Make it a condition of the selection process that the winner of the award cannot sell products and services to the district. This provision will weed out potential conflicts of interest.

When I finally figured this out, the Dallas ISD hired an outstanding firm that executed our expectations with fidelity. They used their processes to gain feedback from students, staff, board members, and community members. They gave status reports on a regular basis and a final report to the senior staff and ultimately to the school board. The plan was thorough and well received. It became the foundational document for the long-range facilities master plan that followed. For the next seven years it became our guidebook as we had to navigate the pandemic. The district was so fortunate that this document was in place as we had to pivot to a full deployment of devices in March 2020.

With the foundational pieces of the technology plan, the facilities master plan was launched. The chief operations officer of the district took the lead in the development of this plan. Consultants who were architects and engineers then evaluated every campus using a facilities condition index (FCI), which had an equity lens. They collected significant data and used it to determine functionality and costs. They determined that at some campuses the renovations would be too costly, and it would be in the best interest of the district to demolish the building and build a new facility. The $3.4 billion bond, the largest bond in the history of Texas, passed in large part due to the processes and documents used in the planning process.

Maintenance in many districts becomes deferred maintenance because it is easy to ignore. Days, weeks, months, and years pass by as neglect consumes the buildings. It becomes very difficult to catch up once slippage occurs. Having a long-range facilities master plan helps quantify the condition of each facility, including costs. In large urban systems the inertia of a complex bureaucracy further exacerbates the inability to resolve issues quickly. Thus, the Core 4 customer service model was ideal to finally solve environmental issues for students and staff in Dallas ISD.

My weekly school visits assisted me in working through the issues and having an objective view of the district's building operations. Driving up to each campus I would focus on the conditions of the grounds, paint, and general cleanliness of the schools. I would consistently remind staff that very few of the neighbors near the campuses had children in the schools but paid property taxes. Why in the world would they vote for a referendum if we did not even care about the appearance of the schools? Inside the building I would walk every corridor assessing the conditions, from the plumbing, to the paint, to the furniture, to the shine on the floors. When the leader exercises this disciplined approach, it rubs off on everyone.

Hinojosa-ism

Under-promise and over-deliver

Manage expectations on goals, time lines, and deliverables. If you do not, then instead of your customers saying "thank you" they will say "it is about time."

Child Nutrition and Food Service

Having an effective child nutrition program has a significant impact on student achievement. Students who do not eat cannot learn. A superintendent should ensure that the chief operating officer pays significant attention to this responsibility. School districts are undoubtedly the largest food service provider in every community. Most students eat breakfast and lunch at school. In some urban communities, especially districts that have extended out of school time, all three weekday meals (breakfast, lunch, and dinner) are provided by schools. A few school districts outsource this responsibility to businesses who specialize in this service, but it is rare.

There are federal requirements in the free and reduced-price lunch (FRPL) program. Household income is the determinant for eligibility. There are very few districts that have a low percentage of students who do not qualify. Most school districts now have over 50 percent of their students who qualify for the program. In many urban districts and inner-ring suburban districts, a super majority of the students qualify, as is also the case in most rural districts.

Childhood obesity is also a significant issue in the United States. Therefore, there have been major shifts in policy regarding child nutrition. In my childhood almost any foods were available for students in schools. In fact, major bottling companies had lucrative contracts with school districts. Even though food preparation and presentation have changed significantly since then, childhood obesity has not. Who is to blame for this crisis? Is it the school, the home, or something in between? The answer is obviously "yes!"

Transportation

State laws exist that identify minimum requirements regarding student transportation to and from schools. Typically, they describe a standard distance from a neighborhood school in which transportation is required. In Texas it is two miles. There is a transportation funding formula that, like special education, is never enough to cover the actual costs. Many of these laws were enacted in a different era. Many of my generation remember walking to school, including me. Today it is extremely rare to see students walking to and from school. Within the two-mile radius there are hazardous routes that include freeways and other major thoroughfares, creeks, and lack of community infrastructure such as sidewalks and streetlights. In many states student enrollment and attendance drive funding. Parents are rightly concerned with the safety of students to and from school. Therefore, many districts transport students above and beyond the required distances.

Logistics and routing are equally challenging in urban, suburban, and rural areas. Traffic, weather, and staffing can create havoc for transportation departments as they can have an unpredictable impact on arrival and dismissal. Recent innovations in GPS and radio-frequency identification (RFID) to track buses can aid, but they are still evolving. Adding complexity is extracurricular activities. Transporting students in and out of the district also creates significant logistical challenges. Working parents who rely on school transportation can lose confidence if the system is inconsistent.

Buses are also expensive and difficult to maintain. Maintaining the fleet on a replacement cycle is often the first item that is cut from the budget because the penalty for doing so is ten years away, the typical life cycle of a bus, and like deferred maintenance it will be someone else's problem to solve. In most states school districts have qualified immunity from legal liabilities except with the use of motor vehicles. The transportation department also cares for the entire maintenance and police vehicles.

Many urban school districts have some form of public-school choice, such as magnet and specialty schools that are beyond the catchment areas of neighborhood schools. To compete for students with private schools, charter schools, home schools, and no school, many districts have become very innovative. But if urban school districts do not provide transportation for choice schools, then students and families really do not have a choice.

Probably the largest issue facing a school transportation department is staffing. This is especially true for bus drivers. The hours are very difficult, and most drivers are part-time employees. You can have the best fleet, logistics, technology, and systems but if you do not have enough staff to execute the transportation plan then it does not matter. This also includes qualified mechanics to fix the fleet, which is constantly under duress.

Various Other Departments

Real Estate

In large systems, a real estate department is critical. These departments must maintain demographic trends and studies. They must work with all jurisdictions to understand the permitting and related requirements. The school district in many cases is the largest landowner in the county. Buying and selling school district properties is complex and there are technical details to follow. In smaller districts, this function tends to be outsourced.

Police and Security

Many large systems in most states have their own commissioned peace officers in the form of a department with a police chief. In Texas, by law, if a district has a police chief the position must report to the superintendent. Some districts have school resource officers that are city police that are assigned to schools. Other districts have unarmed security personnel. With the rash of school shootings in recent years, state legislatures have created more requirements for school systems but many go unfunded.

Legal

Most large urban school systems have legal departments headed by a general counsel. The general counsel is a district employee who reports to the administration but works for the district. Novice superintendents often fail to understand this distinction until there is a conflict with the school board—the general counsel cannot represent you and the school board at the same time. If a significant conflict exists, the general counsel must support the district—not the superintendent. Every superintendent should have their own attorney who represents them and not the district. A general counsel is a generalist and not a specialist in all the specific legal issues that a district must deal with. Thus, outside counsel with expertise in many different disciplines is hired and works for the district on ad hoc issues. Some law firms are so big that they have expertise in virtually all legal matters. On rare occasions, school boards hire a firm just to represent the board. This typically happens when there is a significant rift between the board and the administration. As mentioned previously, most governmental entities have qualified immunity but deal with significant contract and legal matters that require technical legal expertise.

The Big Ideas

Being a successful superintendent means keeping a high-level understanding of operations and digging into the weeds when you need to. Here are the big ideas I shared in Chapter 6:

> ▸ **Don't underestimate the impact of an efficient and effective operations division on the overall academic success of students.**

Operations functions may appear to be mysterious and intimidating but that's only due to lack of familiarity and exposure to business services. My belief is that hungry, humble, and smart leaders can learn enough about these systems to use them to their advantage to improve student academic achievement.

▶ **School districts typically have one of the largest budgets in any community and are one of the largest employers.**
Although you aren't in charge of the finances or the budget, having a strong understanding of how revenue, expenses, and budgeting in your district works is important. And you should work to understand it more deeply and intricately every year you work there. Smart and responsible change can only happen when you have a firm grasp of every dollar that comes in and goes out of your district.

▶ **Create a long-range facilities management plan.**
The plan should include renovation, facilities growth, IT infrastructure, and building management. If you work with a contractor for this plan, it is a good idea to put into the contract that they may not sell any products or services as part of their work with you, so as not to create any conflict of interest. This document then becomes the groundwork to decide what funding sources need to be procured.

CHAPTER #6

Reflect and Act

Now it's time to reflect on what you've read and decide how you can best apply the insights gained from the chapter in practical ways within your district. Use this modified "five 'A's" protocol (Agree, Argue, Apply, Actions, and Accountable) to journal your ideas.

What do you **agree** with in the chapter?	What do you want to **argue** about within the chapter?
How can you **apply** the information from this chapter to your own district?	What **actions** can you take after reading this chapter? And how will you hold yourself **accountable**?

Adapted from Judith Gray, "Four 'A's Text Protocol," National School Reform Faculty (2005), www.nsrfharmony.org.

CHAPTER 7

Cultivate All Endeavors on a Foundation of Ethics and Equity

No leader is perfect. Everyone makes mistakes. I once had a staff member tell me that he was going to be loyal to me. I quickly corrected him and directed him to be loyal to the district and to the students instead. He did not know me, and loyalty is better given to the district and to students rather than to any single person.

The importance of ethics and equity might warrant that this be the first chapter of this book. But I think it is more fitting as the last and most important chapter. I want all superintendents to profoundly reflect on ethics and equity as the foundation of everything we do.

What Do You Believe In?

What we do as leaders demonstrates what we truly believe. What is simple and profound is knowing the difference between right and wrong.

Obvious Ethics

I vividly remember during the first month of my first superintendency I was at a conference in Austin and my attorney noticed that I had an American Express Green Card issued from the district. I joked that as an immigrant, I was proud to have a Green Card. It was my first and only American Express Card, and my attorney made me cut it up in front of him. He had represented only superintendents his entire career, and many of his clients had gotten in trouble because of a district-issued credit card, some by accident and some by design. For the next twenty-seven years, I used my personal cards for all business expenses. By the time I was appointed superintendent of Dallas, my system of business accounting was quite sophisticated. If I requested reimbursement for business expenses, my staff would compile all receipts, double-check them, and then send all documentation to internal audit before it was sent to finance for reimbursement. Monthly, all my expenses were reported to the school board and posted on the district website. As I have noted throughout the book, transparency and accountability are important and this process ensured both.

PRO TIP

Create processes to ensure that all financial transactions are legitimate, documented, double-checked for accuracy, and transparent.

It is not enough, however, to live ethically and make ethically based personal decisions for myself. As a superintendent, I have the responsibility to lead the district ethically as well. For example, early on in my tenure with the Dallas ISD I became aware of a misuse of procurement cards (P-Cards). As I was executing my organic entry plan, I could not help noticing the high volume of Open Record Requests regarding the use of P-Cards from the *Dallas Morning News*. It seemed odd to me that a news organization was making inquiries, so I wanted to learn more. From experience I knew that if proper checks and balances are in place, then the use of a procurement card can expedite securing products and services that campuses and districts can utilize to function efficiently and effectively. But if those systems are not in place, then chaos can ensue. I asked my staff to do an analysis of the information given to the local newspapers. At the time *Dallas Morning News* had three full-time reporters assigned to Dallas ISD, two of them were investigative reporters. My staff let me know that we would be embarrassed by the amount of food that campuses were ordering for staff meals but that would be the extent of the problem. Wow, were they completely wrong. The *News* utilized software to download the data we provided into sophisticated databases and spreadsheets. They hired accountants to review the information and produced some startling reports.

There were virtually no checks and balances in place in the use of the P-Cards. Clerical staff who had very little training were making financial decisions in the name of efficiency. After all, the poor inner-city children deserved the same products and services that suburban students were receiving. Most of the problems were due to sloppy protocols. But the *Dallas Morning News* did an outstanding job of taking the data and writing very juicy long stories with *awful* headlines above the fold every Sunday morning for what seemed like a month. Several principals were fired, and a secretary went to federal prison because she bought a Louis Vuitton purse with her P-Card.

The *Dallas Morning News* subsequently purchased advertising on major billboards that were strategically located on major freeways in and out of downtown Dallas. It is interesting that the location of the billboards purchased were only located on the Dallas North Tollway and North Central Expressway. These were the thoroughfares that led to the only wealth in Dallas, North Dallas and the northern suburbs. It validated the decision of the wealthy to abandon the public schools and ensure segregation in both private and public schools.

All of this happened in my first six months as superintendent. Here I was, the hometown hero, the homeboy coming to save the day, and what a mess I found myself in. However, I did not come in with guns blazing and because of that, Dallas leaders appreciated my collaborative style. Establishing the Dallas Achieves Commission of internal and external stakeholders and meeting individually with the leaders identified in my entry plan—"Who Are the External Stakeholders Critical to Our Future Success?"—bought me some time. The school board fired the auditor and hired a new auditor from out of state. They trusted no one in the state to handle the internal audit function. At the time the best decision I made was to hire a tough former special investigator from the Internal Revenue Service. He convinced me to allow him to set up the Office of Professional Responsibility (OPR). He hired a team of investigators and established protocols for the work. He reported to me directly. It took years and much reform, but eventually the scandals ended. Step by step we created a culture of accountability.

The Buck Stops Here

The divisions and departments that were in the greatest need of transformation reported to me directly. On an ad hoc basis, these included: police, OPR, finance, human resources, technology, school turnaround.

Subtle Breaches of Ethics

Interpersonal trust can be violated in immaterial matters by the behaviors of the leaders. Beyond the obvious inappropriate behavior of a serious nature there are subtleties that are less obvious but erode the effectiveness of leaders. The following is a list of behaviors that are unethical but not always overt and frequently rationalized.

Subtle Unethical Behaviors to Watch Out For

▶ Being untrue to a process or practice that is written or inferred can send a signal that processes and practices are important but only when convenient to the leader.

▶ Loyalty and respect to others indicates how a leader operates. Trust erodes when leaders treat people positively in-person but then denigrate them to others in their absence. This is unethical and sends a message to everyone paying attention that you cannot be trusted.

▶ Being on time is a commitment to an individual or group. Not consistently honoring that commitment speaks volumes.

▶ You have to say what you mean and mean what you say. Failure to do so intimates duplicitous behavior.

▶ People who refuse to admit mistakes are only fooling themselves. Publicly admitting a mistake is very disarming, especially when it is genuine. Modeling this publicly encourages your staff to also admit their mistakes so problem-solving can be addressed immediately.

▶ When leaders profess that they are collaborative and believe in consensus decisions but make command decisions on significant matters, they are signaling their true colors. They are fooling themselves if they think that no one notices. This is part of their body of work.

Consensus Decisions Are More Effective

Command decisions are easy to make—because you make them on your own—but are often hard to implement. Consensus decisions are often messy and can take a long time, but implementation is much deeper and faster because people see their voices in the final product. A way to describe consensus is compromise: I may not like everything in the final decision, but I can live with it.

> ▶ Everyone has lapses in behavior. Everyone falls off the wagon. But how the leader operates over time is a true indicator of their ethical values.

> ▶ Ambition in and of itself is not a bad thing. Most great leaders are very ambitious, but for the greater good. The fake leaders are the ones who have ambition only for themselves and their careers.

> ▶ Leaders who are charismatic can fool some of the people some of the time but not all the people all of the time.

Hinojosa-ism

Good things happen by design, not by accident.

Every system produces the result that it is designed to produce. Things do not just happen randomly.

Equity

The term *equity* has recently become a dirty word through a manufactured crisis. In public education, equity is in part about ethical behavior. Some people want to *be* principal but don't want to *do* principal. Some people want to *be* superintendent but don't want to *do* superintendent. Some people *believe* in racial equity but when it really comes down to it, they don't want to *do* racial equity. They lose their courage when faced with the intensity of the attacks against equitable practices or when they start to feel uncomfortable or when things begin to get too public.

Be ethical in implementing equitable practices. I once attended a racial equity workshop in Dallas ISD where the facilitator had our employees line up by their level of whiteness. I was never so embarrassed. There is no way I could believe that this exercise was going to lead us to improve equity in our district—in fact, it very well might have had a negative effect on our motivation. The district terminated the contract with that consultant. You cannot shame people into doing the right thing. I am very proud of my culture, but I am not a militant. Militants rarely get to the decision-making table and, if they do, they seldom get to stay. My goal is to change the system from within with data and courage. I am not a bomb thrower.

Hinojosa-ism

Some people want to *be* principal but don't want to *do* principal. Some people want to *be* superintendent but don't want to *do* superintendent.

Some people want to have the title but not the responsibility of doing the work required of a leader.

In 2020, the summer after George Floyd was murdered, my senior team and I attended a retreat on racial equity with several large urban districts. There were two main presenters who took two distinct approaches to the topic of equity. The first group made fire and brimstone impassioned speeches to rile up anger in the group. It was classless and unprofessional.

The second presenter, Dr. Ron Ferguson a Massachusetts Institute of Technology (MIT) trained economist, was very clinical and precise, with significant data that convinced some of us that the best way achieve racial equity was to find a way to reach children early on in their lives—from birth to eighteen months of age. The data indicated that by eighteen months the brain was 80 percent developed. Middle-class families understand this and interact with small children to stimulate the mind. Many inner-city Black and Brown children living in poverty do not have the same experience.

PRO TIP

You cannot shame people into doing the right thing.

My team and I had an emergency meeting after the retreat in the hallway of the hotel and developed what I coined Project Legacy 2050. While we are very proud of our Early Learning Strategic

Initiative, waiting until students are three years old is a lost opportunity. We started putting together a guiding coalition of nonprofits,
collective impact groups, the chamber, the hospitals, and anyone who
would listen to us to address the needs of younger children. Our
marketing team thought that Project Legacy 2050 was too clunky and
changed the name to Start Strong Dallas.

Why do I believe in Start Strong Dallas? My wife was an Advanced
Placement English teacher. She read to our sons before they were born. I
used to laugh at her and make fun of her. But our sons became voracious
readers and graduated from Harvard and Princeton even though their
grandparents were immigrants who had a fifth-grade education and
their dad was an immigrant born in a very modest house. One generation removed the cycle of poverty and broke it forever. I know that Dr.
Ron Ferguson and Kitty Taylor Hinojosa are on to something.

It is much better to under-promise and over-deliver in everything
a leader does. Equity is no exception. If you can have data that prove
that you can achieve equity then it will silence the critics, haters, and
bigots. The following initiatives are prime examples of hungry,
humble, and smart people who, with an abundance mentality,
executed on nonlinear projects. These are not miracles. They are
strategic, focused, and well-executed ideas. Fixing a budget problem
is linear. Improving student achievement and addressing racial equity
is not, but it can be done. The following are some specific examples of
equity evident in Dallas ISD.

- When I was hired in 2005, the Texas Education Agency
  cited the school districts for having 1,300 classrooms
  without a certified bilingual teacher. The district traveled to
  Mexico, Puerto Rico, and Spain to recruit teachers. We got
  rid of the existing deficit model bilingual education
  program and replaced it with the abundance model dual
  language program. When I retired, the district had 48
  percent English Learners. Our English Learners are now
  one of our highest-performing student groups. We have
  Black, White, and Latino students (including second and
  third generation) who are biliterate. Dallas has multiple
  high schools offering the seal of biliteracy.

- My team and I made it a strategic initiative and cut other
  programs so that we could afford to launch Start Strong

Dallas. The PreK Strategic Initiative has been significantly successful. We educate three-year-olds for a half day and four-year-olds for a full day. The results have been phenomenal. By the time students in the program reach third grade, they are typically two grade levels ahead academically than students who have not. Ninety-nine percent of those students are students of color.

▶ In 2009, when I was superintendent in Dallas, only 7 percent of students had any kind of postsecondary credential six years after high school. Because of the Pathways in Technology (P-Tech) strategic initiative, when I retired 12 percent of Dallas ISD seniors graduated from high school with an associate degree for free. Ninety-nine percent of those students were students of color.

▶ To create more career opportunities for students, the district created four Career Institutes where students who were not collegebound received externally validated certificates in areas such as aviation, cybersecurity, mechatronics, and dual-language HVAC (heating, ventilation, and air conditioning). Ninety-nine percent of the students enrolled were students of color.

Hinojosa-ism

Effort is good, results are better.

When you are dealing with the lives of children and their future, results matter.

▶ The bond program that raised $3.4 billion for facilities improvements discussed in Chapter 6 had an equity lens. The schools that were moved to the front of the list for renovation were determined by the facility condition index. The bond program identified four schools that were in red-lined areas for customized racial equity support systems for the students, their families, and thus those communities. Ninety-nine percent of those students were students of color.

I have painted a picture showing how ethics and equity are intertwined. It is unethical to have low expectations of students of color. High expectations are good but not enough. High expectations without support is cruelty. Support without expectations is chaos. High expectations with support can achieve racial equity.

Hinojosa-ism

A rising tide lifts all boats. (John F. Kennedy, 1963)

If you take care of the ones most in need, everybody wins.

Strength Bombardment

I want to close with strength bombardment because I love to find strengths and build on them relentlessly—a double dose of love will not hurt you. In the 1990s. I stumbled onto a clinical psychologist from the University of Southern California named Dr. Uvaldo Palomares, who taught me a valuable lesson in human motivation. He invented the Magic Circle. The cornerstone of the circle is an activity called Strength Bombardment. I have used the activity three times per year in a group that has worked together closely for the last twenty-five years. It is extremely powerful.

The culminating activity at the end of an academy or retreat can have a lasting impact on the individuals who participate. It helps people learn to accept compliments and feel confident about their strengths. All the people in the group must sit in a tight circle. It starts with Individual A. Individual B tells A, "The thing I like best about you is . . ." The only thing A can say is "thank you." Then C tells A what it is that C likes about A. The process is repeated until everyone has bombarded A with a description of their strengths. The group then moves on to Individual B and so on until everyone in the group has been bombarded with people articulating their strengths. Sometimes people get emotional because it is so rare to participate in an exercise that builds people up in such a deliberate way.

I hope you try this activity with your staff and the students in your district. I think it will make a profound impact in your district.

The Big Ideas

Being a successful superintendent means keeping ethics and equity at the foundation of who you are. Here are the big ideas I shared in Chapter 7:

- **Strong leaders follow both obvious and subtle ethics.** Having ethical behavior isn't about doing the right thing only when people are looking. It's about consistently living by ethical behavior in your personal and professional life. Don't be afraid to make mistakes and admit when you do. How a leader operates over time is the true indicator of their ethical values.

- **Equity doesn't happen by accident—it's intentional.** As leaders, we can't just hope that equity practices will happen across our district. Everyone must be responsible for implementing them, and it starts with you.

- **We are all better when we start with our strengths.** When we look for strengths in one another and encourage each other to build on them, we all make growth together. This changes our thinking from a deficit model to one of asset thinking and allows us to embrace ourselves unapologetically for who we are!

CHAPTER #7

Reflect and Act

Now it's time to reflect on what you've read and decide how you can best apply the insights gained from the chapter in practical ways within your district. Use this modified "five 'A's" protocol (Agree, Argue, Apply, Actions, and Accountable) to journal your ideas.

What do you **agree** with in the chapter?	What do you want to **argue** about within the chapter?
How can you **apply** the information from this chapter to your own district?	What **actions** can you take after reading this chapter? And how will you hold yourself **accountable**?

Adapted from Judith Gray, "Four 'A's Text Protocol," National School Reform Faculty (2005), www.nsrfharmony.org.

Conclusion

If you are a veteran successful superintendent, I hope you have found a few nuggets here to reflect on your experiences. We have all lived in this world, and the job is not linear. I am sure you have experienced some things that were surreal. I know I have said this often, but we cannot make this stuff up.

If you are a novice superintendent, it is my expectation that you have also found some nuggets of information that will help you avoid some of the pitfalls in this job. Being a superintendent is a great profession because you can make a significant impact on the academic success of students. However, you cannot do the job if you cannot stay in the job. You must have a mindset of perseverance. The students, board, staff, and community depend on you.

If you are an aspiring superintendent, my goal is not for you to be able to get a job. My goal is to give you knowledge and skills to be successful in superintendency. But the most important attribute is your attitude. You have to *do* you, but it is not *about* you. It's about having the tools you need to support your staff, affect positive change in the community, and nurture academic excellence in your students.

Hinojosa-ism

The best way to predict the future is to create it.

I look to the future with hope and aspiration. An optimistic person believes they can control their destiny. Great leaders control the future for all who follow them.

References

Gray, J. (2005). *Four 'A's text protocol*. National School Reform Faculty. www.nsrfharmony.org

Great City Schools. (2021, June). *Mirrors or windows*. https://www.cgcs.org/Page/1288

Kennedy, J. (1962, August 17). *Remarks in Pueblo, Colorado following approval of the Frying Pan-Arkansas Project (336)*. Public Papers of the Presidents: John F. Kennedy.

Index

A Sage Company

CORWIN HAS ONE MISSION: to enhance education through intentional professional learning.

We build long-term relationships with our authors, educators, clients, and associations who partner with us to develop and continuously improve the best evidence-based practices that establish and support lifelong learning.

Solutions YOU WANT | *Experts* YOU TRUST | *Results* YOU NEED

INSTITUTES

Corwin Institutes provide regional and virtual events where educators collaborate with peers and learn from industry experts. Prepare to be recharged and motivated!

corwin.com/institutes

ON-SITE PROFESSIONAL LEARNING

Corwin on-site PD is delivered through high-energy keynotes, practical workshops, and custom coaching services designed to support knowledge development and implementation.

www.corwin.com/pd

VIRTUAL PROFESSIONAL LEARNING

Our virtual PD combines live expert facilitation with the flexibility of anytime, anywhere professional learning. See the power of intentionally designed virtual PD.

www.corwin.com/virtualworkshops

CORWIN ONLINE

Online learning designed to engage, inform, challenge, and inspire. Our courses offer practical, classroom-focused instruction that will meet your continuing education needs and enhance your practice.

www.corwinonline.com

PLSN209YA8

Visit www.corwin.com

C**O**RWIN

Made in the USA
Middletown, DE
09 June 2025

76733170R00086